More praise for *Ethical Intelligence*

"Dr. Weinstein shows how ethical intelligence is an essential component of the good life. I love this book!"

— Denise Austin, fitness expert and author of *Get Energy!*

"*Ethical Intelligence* will help you make smart decisions everywhere you go. And it's not just for business leaders; it's for everyone."

— Deborah Norville, TV personality and author of
The Power of Respect

ETHICAL INTELLIGENCE

OTHER BOOKS BY DR. BRUCE WEINSTEIN

AS EDITOR

Ethics in the Hospital Setting

Dental Ethics

Ethical Issues in Pharmacy

AS AUTHOR

What Should I Do?
4 Simple Steps to Making Better Decisions in Everyday Life

Life Principles: Feeling Good by Doing Good

Is It Still Cheating If I Don't Get Caught? (for young adults)

ETHICAL INTELLIGENCE

Five Principles for Untangling
Your Toughest Problems
at Work and Beyond

BRUCE WEINSTEIN, PhD
The Ethics Guy®

New World Library
Novato, California

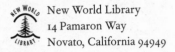 New World Library
14 Pamaron Way
Novato, California 94949

Please note that nothing in this book should be considered legal or psychological advice.

The stories are true or are based on events that happened. In some cases, the author has changed names and other details to protect confidentiality.

A different version of some of this material appeared in Bloomberg Businessweek Online.

Text design by Tona Pearce Myers

Library of Congress Cataloging-in-Publication Data
Weinstein, Bruce D.
Ethical intelligence : five principles for untangling your toughest problems at work and beyond / Bruce Weinstein.
    p.   cm.
Includes bibliographical references and index.
ISBN 978-1-60868-054-2 (pbk. : alk. paper)
1. Applied ethics. 2. Business ethics. I. Title.
BJ1031.W38 2011
170—dc23   2011028707

First printing, October 2011
ISBN 978-1-60868-054-2
Printed in Canada on 100% postconsumer-waste recycled paper

New World Library is a proud member of the Green Press Initiative.

10 9 8 7 6 5 4 3 2 1

For Ed Askinazi, Jeff Clarkson, Will Hood, and B. David Joffe —
four terrific, lifelong, and ethically intelligent friends

Contents

PART 3

Ethical Intelligence in Your Personal Life

PART I

Understanding the Five Principles
of Ethical Intelligence

CHAPTER I

Introducing the Principles

How ethically intelligent are you? Take the quiz below, then read on. In this chapter and the two that follow, you will learn the five principles of ethical intelligence and discover your ethics IQ.

ETHICS QUIZ

1. You notice that your friend Heather has posted a new picture of herself on Facebook in which she is smoking a bong with one hand and holding a bottle of vodka in the other. What would you do?

   A. Tell her you don't think this photo is a good idea.
   B. Don't say anything about it to her.
   C. "Like" the photo.
   D. Copy the photo to your hard drive and use it against her if she ever double-crosses you.

2. You're having lunch at a restaurant and overhear two colleagues, Bob and Ray, talking about a client with whom your business is having difficulty. They mention the client by name as well as specific information about the problem. What would you do?

    A. Approach them and mention your concerns about confidentiality.

    B. Ignore it.

    C. Tell your supervisor what you witnessed.

    D. Record your colleagues with your cell phone's video camera and post the clip on YouTube.

3. You take your twelve-year-old son to the movies. At the box office, you see a sign that says, "Children up to eleven: $6.00. Adults: $12.00." The movie theater's management thus considers your son to be an adult. What would you do?

    A. Ask for one adult and one child ticket.

    B. Ask for two adult tickets.

    C. Give your son the money and have him ask for a ticket.

    D. Ask your son what he thinks you should do, and then do whatever he suggests.

4. An employee you supervise comes to work late, spends a lot of time shopping online, takes long lunches and coffee breaks, and leaves early. A few months ago, you fired someone for doing the same thing. This person, however, is the daughter of a close personal friend. You've talked with her several times about her conduct, but the problems continue. What would you do?

    A. Fire her.

    B. Ignore it.

    C. Talk with her again and tell her this is her last chance to straighten up.

    D. Ask your friend (her parent) to talk with her.

5. You wake up on a workday with the flu. What would you do?

    A. Stay at home and rest.

    B. Stay at home and work.

C. Go to work but avoid socializing with people.

D. Go to work but socialize only with the people you don't like.

DIFFERENT CHOICES, DIFFERENT REASONS

Now that you've made your selections, on what basis did you make them? Which of the following guided your selections?

- How you imagined feeling in each scenario
- The way you've acted in similar situations in the past and what happened as a result
- What you were taught was right and wrong
- What you understand is expected of you as a member of your religious tradition
- How you might stand to benefit from each possible option
- What others would think of you if they knew you'd made one choice over another

If you present the quiz to a group of your friends and coworkers, you'll probably find a range of responses to each scenario. Also, the reasons people give for making their choices may be different from yours, even if you made the same choices. For example, both you and a coworker might choose to stay home and rest when you wake up with the flu, but your reason might be, "I don't want to make other people sick," whereas your coworker's justification could be, "Any day I don't have to go in to the office is fine with me."

Whatever choices you've made, you probably believe that yours were the best ones. (Otherwise, why would you have made them?) But how do you reconcile this with the fact that other people you like and trust might make different choices in the same scenarios or have different reasons for making the same choices? They're good people, but each one believes that his or her choices (and reasons) are the best ones, even though they may be different from yours. How can we tell what the best solutions actually are, no matter who is looking at the problem?

The answer lies in five simple principles:

1. Do No Harm
2. Make Things Better
3. Respect Others
4. Be Fair
5. Be Loving

There are several things worth noting about these principles:

- You know these principles already.
- They're the basis of both religious traditions and secular societies.
- They're tremendously difficult to live by.

When you were young, you learned these principles from your parents and teachers. If you went to Sunday school, the principles were taught in every class you took. If you were a member of a civic organization such as the Boy or Girl Scouts, or the 4-H, Optimist, Rotary, or Kiwanis clubs, these principles guided just about everything you did there.

But the five principles above aren't just for kids. As Jeffrey Moses illustrates in his book *Oneness: Great Principles Shared by All Religions*,[1] the principles are the bedrock of Eastern and Western religious traditions alike. Indeed, it's hard to imagine how any society or culture could fail to honor these principles; you'd be afraid to leave your house, for example, if Do No Harm did not guide the behavior of your fellow citizens. All five principles are the glue that binds us together as a nation, as persons of faith, and in every relationship we have or are likely to have.

In spite of their central role in everyday life, it's easy to forget how important they are and to act instead on impulses that beckon us but that may, in the long run, be more hurtful than helpful.

Suppose, for example, that you're driving down the highway one afternoon and the driver behind you starts flashing his lights and honking his horn in an effort to get you to speed up. But you're already traveling at the speed limit, and you're not even in the fast lane. There is no good reason to go faster than you already are, so you ignore him.

All of a sudden, he moves over, rushes by you, makes an obscene gesture, and appears to mutter something nasty. It's tempting to return the gesture, flash your lights at him, and even roll your window down and curse back at him. But what would the consequences of this decision be? Most likely, you would:

- Feel worse, not better
- Make the other driver feel worse, not better
- Increase the risk of injury or death to you and those around you
- Risk getting pulled over by a police officer
- Set a poor example of how to respond to difficult situations, if anyone (especially your child) is in the car with you

It's understandable that you'd want to return one rude gesture with another, and I know I'm not the only one who has given in to this impulse on occasion. But it's one thing to understand the impulse and quite another to justify acting on it. Giving him "a taste of his own medicine" in the above situation may harm all concerned — including you and fellow drivers who have no stake in the matter and deserve to be able to travel safely.

Thus, if you look at the situation objectively, it would be wrong to do something that would make things worse. You might not be able to get the hostile driver to calm down, but you can surely avoid causing harm to him, yourself, your passengers, and other drivers. The first principle, Do No Harm, shows you the best way to respond in this situation.

In fact, all five principles mentioned above provide excellent guidelines for making the best possible decisions in every area of your life. These principles have legal, financial, and psychological implications; but they are first and foremost principles of ethics, and they form the core of what I call "ethical intelligence." In this book, I will show you how to enhance your ethical intelligence by mastering these principles, so that you'll be equipped to make the right decisions at work and in your personal life.

First, let's see how ethical intelligence differs from its close cousin, emotional intelligence.

ETHICAL INTELLIGENCE
VERSUS EMOTIONAL INTELLIGENCE

In 1995, a psychologist and science journalist named Daniel Goleman shook up the world with his book *Emotional Intelligence*.[2] Goleman described an indispensable element of professional and personal success: the ability to discern how others are feeling, which can be quite different from the ways they present themselves to the world.

Suppose, for example, that you and I know each other well and we meet for coffee one day. You ask me how I'm doing, and I say, "I'm fine." But several signs suggest I'm anything but fine: I avoid eye contact, which is unusual for me; my voice is quieter than it normally is; I'm not smiling, which isn't like me; and I seem unusually distracted. It is your emotional intelligence that enables you to notice these signs and to correctly conclude that I'm not fine at all. Someone who doesn't possess your level of emotional intelligence (or any at all) wouldn't notice that something is amiss when we meet.

But now comes a tough question: What should you do? The answer isn't obvious. Is it better to mention the fact that I don't seem all right to you, or should you just ignore it? If our chat over coffee doesn't give you any useful information about what's really going on, would it be right to follow up with a phone call or email, or simply say to yourself, "He's an adult, and if he wants to tell me what's going on, he will"? Emotional intelligence alone won't — and can't — tell you what you ought to do. That's because emotional intelligence is a *psychological* matter, but the question "What's the right thing to do?" is an *ethical* one. To be fully human, it's not enough to have emotional intelligence. We need ethical intelligence, too.

Let's take a closer look at the five principles that form the core of ethical intelligence, and then we'll consider how they can help us determine the right way to tackle the problems from the beginning of this chapter.

SUMMARY

The five principles of ethical intelligence are:

1. Do No Harm
2. Make Things Better
3. Respect Others
4. Be Fair
5. Be Loving

As the quiz that opened this chapter suggests, it's not always easy to do the right thing, or even to know what the right thing is. The principles of ethical intelligence provide the foundation for making the right choices in every area of your life.

CHAPTER 2

The Five Principles of Ethical Intelligence

Now that we've identified the five principles of ethical intelligence, let's examine them one by one, with an eye toward understanding how they imbue your life with meaning and enrich all of your relationships.

PRINCIPLE I: DO NO HARM

You may remember playing the party game "telephone" when you were a child: someone whispers a phrase or short statement to you, which you then whisper to someone else, who tells yet another person. After the message has been passed to a few more people, you discover that it bears little resemblance to its original form. When you're a kid, it's fun to notice this shift, and it's always good for a laugh.

But we also play the game as adults all the time, even if we don't recognize it as such, and with social networking technology, it's easier than ever to do this. The effects, however, can damage businesses, careers, and lives. Consider this: On February 8, 2009, a Twitter subscriber tweeted that a man driving a silver truck had kidnapped a young girl, and the tweet included the truck's license plate information. An Amber Alert (which signifies that a child has been abducted) went out from Salt Lake City all the way to Oklahoma, putting both law enforcement and citizens on the lookout for the truck. The only thing true about the tweet, however, was the license plate ID and the description of the car it belonged to.[1] You can just imagine how the driver felt upon learning of this vicious and baseless attack. Even if the tweeter meant no harm by the prank or somehow found it funny, the power of the Internet turned the "joke" into a multistate, reputation-damaging scandal and an abuse of public resources.

The good news about the Do No Harm principle of ethical intelligence is that all you need to do to apply it is — nothing! Do No Harm is largely a principle of restraint. When you choose not to respond to a nasty gesture with more of the same, you're applying Do No Harm. When you choose not to pass along rumor or gossip, you're applying Do No Harm. When you decide not to use a knife to open those ridiculous plastic clamshell packages that encase so many products these days, you're wisely forgoing an action that would likely send you reeling in pain to the emergency room. Here, too, you're applying Do No Harm.

Speaking of the hospital, Do No Harm is usually associated with health-care professionals. Medical, nursing, pharmacy, and dental students are taught this principle early in their training, and for good reason: when you're sick, you hope that your health-care providers will help you get better, but you rightly expect that they won't make you worse.

When you think about it, though, Do No Harm applies not just to physicians, nurses, dentists, pharmacists, and clinical social workers but also to attorneys, accountants, TV news producers, construction workers, teachers, students — everyone. The very least you can expect from your fellow human beings is their willingness not to inflict physical or emotional damage on you, and of course, they have a right to insist that you do the same for them.

It's true that people do just the opposite all the time, but they do so wrongfully; and depending on the nature of the harm caused, punishment is in order. To be a decent human being and to live in a civil society require a commitment to the first principle of ethical intelligence.

What Exactly Is Harm?

I use the term *harm* to refer to any type of action that damages others. These actions range in severity from mild pain or discomfort to severe distress and — the ultimate harm — loss of life. Generally speaking, harm is not the same as offense. When I was in Berlin many years ago as a graduate student, I recall seeing a marquee for a porn film whose title was written in large letters and could not have been more explicit. Many people would find this offensive, yet it's a stretch to say that display was harmful. Of course, it's a good thing to avoid causing offense as well as causing harm. But from an ethical point of view, we will focus on harm because it cuts deeper.

There are a few corollaries to Do No Harm that are worth mentioning: Prevent Harm and Minimize Unavoidable Harm. Let's look at each of these in turn.

Prevent Harm

As we've seen, Do No Harm is a principle of nonintervention. If you're tempted to do or say something hurtful, the ethically intelligent response is to restrain that impulse, as difficult as that can be. When you become aware of an imminent harm to others or yourself, however, you are called upon to do something rather than nothing. Preventing harm is an essential element of ethical intelligence.

The classic example of preventing harm to others is arranging for someone who has had too much to drink to get a ride home. Lifeguards who dive into a pool to save someone from drowning are also putting this idea into practice. But preventing harm isn't limited to parties, pub crawls, or swimming pools, and the potential harm doesn't have to be death or dismemberment. When my wife and I moved into our current apartment, we were told not to keep wet umbrellas or snow boots outside our door. This seemed like an extreme attempt to keep the hallways clean, until we learned that this measure was necessary to prevent our neighbors from slipping and falling. Preventing harm to others doesn't even have to involve people. When you carefully choose the kind of toys you allow your pets to play with, you're applying this rule.

When we revisit the ethics quiz, we'll see how the duty to prevent harm applies to such diverse scenarios as waking up with the flu, overhearing colleagues discussing a client in public, and seeing that a Facebook friend has posted a picture of herself smoking pot. For now, the main thing to keep in mind about this first corollary to the Do No Harm principle of ethical intelligence is that it involves doing *something* rather than *nothing* when harm is likely to occur to people you know and care about (and even those you don't know or like).[2]

Minimize Unavoidable Harm

Let's face it: there are times you have to do things that you know will hurt people. When you're breaking up with someone, downsizing your department, or punishing your kids, there is no way around the fact that your actions will be hurtful to others (or will at least seem hurtful to them). In these situations, ethical intelligence calls upon you to ask, "How can I minimize harm that is unavoidable?"

When I was single, I had plenty of first dates that were also last dates. Sometimes it was clear to both of us right away that it wasn't going to work, and sometimes one of us wasn't attracted to the other. In the second case, typically the uninterested one simply didn't respond to the other person's calls or emails. But was this the ethically intelligent way to handle the matter? No, because it made a bad situation worse. The spurned party was forced to wonder, "What happened? Did I do something wrong?" The sting of being rejected doubtless stung for longer than it should have.

June, a woman I went out with three times, demonstrated ethical intelligence on our third date. She said, "I'm sorry, but I just don't feel a spark." I was disappointed that she wasn't interested, but I appreciated the fact that she had the courage to tell me directly that she didn't want to pursue a relationship. Of all the dates that didn't work out, this experience with June hurt the least, because she acted with ethical intelligence.

In the next chapter, I'll talk about better and worse ways to criticize someone and let someone go. For now, let's turn our attention to the second principle that ethically intelligent people live by.

PRINCIPLE 2: MAKE THINGS BETTER

Why did you choose to do what you do for a living? Was it because you wanted to become rich? Famous? Well liked? You may have achieved some or all of these goals, but I'll bet that none of these were what you were really after. Instead, you're in your line of work mainly because you wanted to make a positive difference in some way. Perhaps you wanted to improve the customer experience or your own family's situation. Maybe your goal was to shake up the world with an idea — an invention or a much-needed service that wasn't being provided. Or as an artist, you wanted to touch people with a song, a painting, a novel, or a screenplay. Every time you provide excellent service to a client, develop your entrepreneurship, write a story, or take your son to his music lessons, you're making things better for the people in your life and for those you don't even know.

But do you also take time every day to make things better for *yourself*? Do you make sure to have three nutritious meals? Work out or go for a walk? Meditate, nap, or play?

Ethically intelligent people do. Ethics isn't just about how you treat other people. It's also about how you treat yourself. Regarding yourself in an ethical manner means making sure that your body, mind, and spirit are nourished and satisfied.

Flight attendants tell us, "Should the cabin lose pressure, oxygen masks will drop down from the overhead area. Please put one over your own mouth before you attempt to help others." Why? Because the only way we can hope to be of service to others is if we're in good shape ourselves.

But the reason to make things better for yourself is not just because you need to be in tip-top shape to serve others but also because you should treat yourself with dignity. It's a simple argument, really:

PREMISE. Ethics is about treating people appropriately.

PREMISE. You're a person.

CONCLUSION. Ethics includes treating yourself appropriately.

I don't mean to trivialize the issue of self-regarding duties. It's an issue that has been, and continues to be, the subject of rich, lively philosophical debate (the University of Chicago Press's journal *Ethics*, for example, published a series of articles on the topic in the early 1960s). But if you accept the two premises above, the conclusion is inescapable.

It's worth noting that principle 2 shows how ethics demands more of us than the law does. You're not legally required to make things better for others or yourself. But ethical intelligence does require this.

PRINCIPLE 3: RESPECT OTHERS

Aretha sings about it. Eminem raps about it. Parents tell their children how important it is. But what does respect have to do with ethical intelligence? Isn't respect just a matter of etiquette?

Not entirely. It's true that when a dinner guest arrives empty handed, stays too long, and leaves your bathroom a mess, that person has disrespected you through his or her poor manners. But there are other aspects of respect that are squarely within the realm of ethics because they touch upon the things that matter most. It's one thing for a dinner guest to chew with his mouth open; it's another thing for him to tell everyone about a private conversation you had, steal money from the wallet you left lying around, or describe the contents of your medicine cabinet to his four thousand followers on Twitter. All of these acts are disrespectful, but the second set cuts more deeply and causes greater damage. Rude or offensive behavior is a breach of etiquette. Behavior that is harmful or violates another person's rights is a breach of ethics.

Ethically intelligent people show respect in the deeper sense by honoring the values, preferences, and, most important, the rights of others. "Do unto others as they would have you do unto them" is another way of putting it.[3] Note that this sounds like the Golden Rule, "Do unto others as you would have them do unto you," but it's not exactly that.

Ooooweee, Pepperoni — My Favorite!

Suppose your friend Gene invites you and three mutual friends over for a casual dinner party. When you arrive, you smell the aroma of five piping hot pepperoni pizzas. "Come and get 'em!" Gene says as he opens the gooey cardboard boxes. Gene, as everyone who knows him can attest, loves meat. But two of the people in the group are vegetarians. One is a vegetarian for health reasons, and another believes that it's unethical to eat animals. Has Gene done anything wrong? Not according to the Golden Rule, because he has treated his friends the way he would like to be treated. But Gene *has* done something wrong since he didn't bother finding out what would be pleasing to anyone else. He assumed not only that his friends share his food preferences but that they also share his values about what is healthful or acceptable to eat. To show respect for people, especially friends, means taking the time to find out what they like and don't like, rather than just assuming they'll like what you like. In other words, respect in the deepest, most meaningful sense means treating you as an autonomous individual whose preferences and even values may be different from mine.

You could argue that vegetarians, people with food allergies, and those with special needs have a responsibility to inform their hosts of these dietary restrictions in advance. If you want to have your needs respected, it helps to make others aware of those needs. But failing to do so doesn't let the other person in the relationship off the hook. Gene's pizza party was fun for Gene, but because he didn't take the time to find out what his guests would want or need, he failed to act with ethical intelligence. It is the thought that counts, and Gene didn't think this one through.

All of this seems so complicated. Do we really have to know the intricate details of everyone's idiosyncratic values and preferences to be able to show respect for them? No. Even if I don't know you very well, I can safely assume that you'd expect me to do the following things on your behalf: keep private things private, tell you the truth, and keep my promises to you. We'll examine each in turn, but it's worth taking a look at a complex topic that is at the heart of the third principle of ethical intelligence: rights.

What Are Rights, and Where Do They Come From?

A right is an entitlement. It is fundamentally different from a wish, desire, or dream. If you have a right to x, then someone else has an obligation to give you x. Suppose x stands for "being paid to do your job." If you have a right to be paid to do your job, then the person employing you has an obligation to pay you when you do your job. Of course, there is a limit to what you can legitimately claim as a right. You might like to have a hot fudge sundae with whipped cream, walnuts, and an all-natural cherry on top — who wouldn't? — but unless it has been promised to you, you could hardly say you have a right to it. Since you're not entitled to it, others have no obligation to give it to you.

Rights speak to the inherent dignity in human beings (and, many would add, all living beings). They are at the core not just of the third principle of ethical intelligence, as I'll show in a moment, but of ethical intelligence in general. The most obvious problem with the concept of rights has to do with their origin. Where do they come from?

In his last HBO special, *It's Bad for Ya*, George Carlin pokes fun at the notion of rights.[4] He claims that people made them up, and to support this statement, he notes that different countries have different lists of rights; some don't officially consider anything to be a right. With so much confusion about the issue, Carlin's conclusion is that all we have are privileges, which can be taken away by the decision of whoever happens to be in power.

But Carlin fails to distinguish between a legal right and an ethical one. He is correct that legal rights are subject to the whims of one's government, and they can (and do) change from time to time and place to place. But ethical rights don't. They are the basis of legal rights, and they exist even when not codified by law. For example, in most countries, child pornography is not a crime, but in the United States, it is.[5] Children have a legal right not to be sexually exploited in this country; they have no such right in Ethiopia, Thailand, or Iran.[6] Can we conclude from this fact that children in the United States are entitled not to be abused but that elsewhere it's okay to abuse them? The answer, of course, is no. A child's right not to become fodder for pedophiles comes from his or her inherent dignity, which commands our respect whether or not there are laws that make this official. Rights in the ethical sense speak to what we are owed simply by virtue of being human.

For the remainder of the book, then, I shall use *right* in the ethical sense, not the legal sense, and I will take it on faith that you and I both accept the premise that we have a right to be treated with respect and that we have a responsibility to treat others with respect, too.

In chapter 4, I'll explore more deeply the difference between ethics and the law. But for now, let's get back to the third principle of ethical intelligence, Respect Others, and how it applies to the issues of confidentiality, truth telling, and promise keeping.

Confidentiality

I was once in a hospital elevator and overheard two doctors talking about a patient. They mentioned the patient's full name as well as the fact that he'd just had a quadruple cardiac bypass. I knew the person they were talking about but didn't know that he'd had surgery. I didn't even know he had a health problem. I wondered, "Should I send the fellow a get-well card? What if he asks me how I knew that he was convalescing?" I couldn't very well tell him, "I heard your doctors talking about you in an elevator at the hospital."

When we discuss confidential information in public, we betray the trust that someone has placed in us to keep private information private. It is nothing less than an act of theft. The doctors I encountered weren't bad people, and I'm sure they didn't intend to breach their patient's right to privacy. But their conversation in that small public space nevertheless was inconsistent with ethical intelligence.

The ethically intelligent person respects confidential information and does his or her level best to protect it.[7]

Truth Telling

A dear friend of mine named Maurice brought a bottle of wine to a party at my home. I took one sip and immediately spit it out. "Yech," I said. "It tastes like battery acid!" Ordinarily, I wouldn't have said such a crass thing; but my friend loves a good joke, and I figured he'd like this one. Besides, I was telling the truth. What could be wrong with that?

A lot, as it turned out. Maurice was hurt by my declaration, and I found myself apologizing over and over for my poor judgment. I learned the hard way: telling the truth isn't always such an admirable thing. My friend hadn't even asked me what I thought of the wine, but if he had, it would have been better to say something truthful that wouldn't have been hurtful, such as, "It was very nice of you to bring us a bottle of wine, Maurice. Unnecessary, but much appreciated!" I would have been able to honor both the duty to tell the truth (entailed by the third principle of ethical intelligence) and the duty to avoid hurting my friend's feelings and our relationship (entailed by the first principle of ethical intelligence).

One of the challenges in ethical intelligence is knowing how truthful to be, since telling the truth, the whole truth, and nothing but the truth in every situation can harm valued relationships.[8] When you're giving testimony in a legal deposition, you have both a legal and an ethical obligation to be completely truthful. The ethically intelligent taxpayer tells the IRS the truth about his or her income, even though he or she could save some money by fudging this information. When they make a mistake at work, ethically intelligent people fess up to their bosses rather than blame someone or something else. In all of these scenarios, ethical intelligence calls for being forthright about the truth.

Outside of such circumstances, however, ethical intelligence requires balancing the responsibilities of telling the truth and not causing harm. It's true that Maurice's bottle of wine was foul tasting, but I was under no obligation to tell him this. In fact, it's just the opposite: I was wrong to do so. Striking the right balance between being truthful and not hurting people is what makes living with ethical intelligence so challenging — and ultimately, so rewarding.

A final word about balancing truth telling with doing no harm: Earlier I distinguished offense from harm and said that our discussion of ethical intelligence would be concerned only with harm. But isn't what I said to Maurice about his gift more akin to offense than harm? How did I damage Maurice in any significant way?

The harm that followed from my poor choice of words wasn't to Maurice per se but to our relationship. Our friendship has endured (and it would have been a mighty shaky one if a single slip of the tongue could ruin it). But words or actions that are merely offensive can harm a valued relationship, especially if this occurs often enough, the words or actions are particularly egregious, or the person on the receiving end is highly sensitive. Good relationships are characterized by mutual respect and trust; offensive speech can compromise this. Such speech thus falls within the purview of ethical intelligence (or unintelligence, as the case may be). Telling the truth to someone should take into account the degree to which your relationship could be harmed by what you say.

It's time to look at a third crucial component of respecting others: honoring the promises you make.

Promise Keeping

You know that friend you have who keeps breaking appointments with you? The two of you make plans to have lunch or meet for coffee, but at the last minute, your friend calls or texts to say he or she can't make it. The reason may be plausible, and things do come up from time to time; but when someone habitually reneges on a promise, it feels as though that person doesn't really respect you. That's because he or she doesn't really respect you. The third principle, Respect Others, addresses the importance of being true to our word.

In 2008, the company that owned the Dr Pepper brand promised a free can of its signature soda to "every American" if the rock group Guns N' Roses released its long-gestating album *Chinese Democracy* by the end of the year. The management may have reasoned that because the record's release had been delayed for so long, it was highly unlikely that the company would have to make good on its promise. But when Guns N' Roses frontman Axl Rose surprised the music world by completing the work and putting it out before the end of the year, Dr Pepper was deluged with requests for a complimentary drink and initially couldn't meet the demand. The media presented the story as a public relations debacle, but the issue was really an ethical one: the company made a promise it couldn't keep (at least at first). Its website crashed under the weight of far more visits than the company had anticipated, and many people were frustrated by their inability to get the free sodas they'd been told they would get.[9]

Eventually, things worked out, but the incident does present a valuable lesson: keep the promises you make, and don't make promises you're not prepared to keep. We may not always be able to do this — it can be difficult to honor a promise when something better comes along, and it's not always possible to predict how many people will take you up on an offer you make in good faith — but striving to be true to one's word is an essential element of ethical intelligence.[10]

The third principle of ethical intelligence, Respect Others, is founded on the idea that human beings ought to treat one another as ends in themselves and not merely as a means to an end.[11] When you keep a friend's confidence, or tell a client the truth about your products and services, or uphold a promise you've made to your spouse, you honor that person's right to be treated with respect, and you honor the dignity of two people — the other person and yourself.

PRINCIPLE 4: BE FAIR

In an episode of *The Andy Griffith Show* called "A Medal for Opie," Ron (at the time, Ronny) Howard's character decides he wants to win an upcoming foot race. He practices hard for days with Barney. He fantasizes about a stadium filled with people cheering him on as he is awarded the first-place prize. But on the day of the race, out of four contestants, he comes in fourth. He mopes back to his house all alone and spends the afternoon feeling sorry for himself. When his father arrives, he tells Opie that it wasn't very nice of him to walk away without congratulating the winner.

"I didn't win!" Opie replies.

That's true, his dad tells him, but the important thing is that he was in there trying. "It's nice to win something," Andy says, "but it's more important to know how not to win something." It takes courage to be a good loser, Andy stresses, and he implores his son several times to graciously acknowledge the other boy's victory.

But Opie won't hear of it, and you can feel Andy's growing anger at his son's stubbornness.

So how does Andy resolve the impasse? Take Opie kicking and screaming out to the woodshed for a spanking? Send him to bed without supper? Carry him out to the car and drive him over to the winner's house for a forced apology?

None of these things. Andy's solution is much more powerful:

he ends the discussion by saying, very slowly so that each word is not only heard but felt, "All right, that's the way it's going to be, as long as we understand one another."

And then comes the kicker: "But I want you to know one thing. I'm *disappointed* in you."

End of scene. Cut to commercial.

What do you think happens next? If this show were made today, we'd probably see Opie getting ready for the next race, training even harder, and leaving the other kids in the dust as he takes the first-place medal. But Frank Tarloff, the writer of the episode, wisely chose to make the climax of the story not about winning (which would have undercut the message of the previous scene) but about what it means to discipline a child appropriately. The story's conclusion is a single scene in which a despondent Opie walks into his father's office, throws his arms around his dad, and says tearfully, "Paw, I don't want you to be disappointed in me." They hug each other, and the episode ends.

We never see Opie run another race, but we know that he has been changed forever by what his father has said and the way he said it.

I can think of no better example in TV (or film, for that matter) that shows how to discipline someone fairly. It's only natural to be upset when someone you care about doesn't do something he or she ought to do, or does something he or she shouldn't have done. We appreciate Andy's growing anger at his son's refusal to be a good sport. But Andy doesn't let this emotion get the best of him. He modulates his anger and uses it to help Opie become a better person, which is (or should be) the goal of discipline. To be fair is to give others their due, and when it comes to disciplining someone, what is due is neither an extreme display of anger nor an absence of it. What's due is the right amount of it. Andy Taylor's reaction to

Opie's behavior prompts the boy to get back on track and is a powerful illustration of ethical intelligence in action.[12]

Fairness and Ethical Intelligence

I love the Beatles — who doesn't? — but John Lennon was wrong when he sang, "All you need is love." To be fully human, and to live your life with ethical intelligence, you need more than love. You need to treat people fairly, too. What constitutes fairness, of course, has been, and will continue to be, fiercely debated. But the essence of fairness is beyond dispute: it is about *giving others their due*.[13] Of particular importance in ethical intelligence are these three areas of giving others their due:

- Allocating scarce resources
- Disciplining or punishing
- Rectifying injustice

Let's examine each in turn.

Allocating Scarce Resources

"If you don't manage your time, someone else will." This sensible rule is the cornerstone of time management books and seminars, and no one can hope to be successful — in business or anywhere else — without organizing one's schedule wisely. But time management isn't really about management; it's about fairness. It's about how to properly allocate the most precious commodity of all. Time is the only thing that you are guaranteed to have a limited supply of and that keeps getting more and more limited, no matter what you do.

When you spend more time on a project than is warranted, that's not unfortunate; it's unfair. When you don't spend enough time with your family and friends, that is also unfair. When you overlook giving yourself enough time to take care of your own needs, you're being unfair. Making sure that you give everyone in your life, including yourself, what you owe is a crucial component of ethical intelligence.

When we ask who should get a liver transplant when there aren't enough donors, we're not asking a medical question; we're asking an ethical one. By the same token, when you ask yourself, "What should I do first on my overstuffed to-do list?" you're not asking a strategic question; you're asking an ethical one. To manage your time well is to make ethically intelligent decisions, and this means doing the best you can to allocate the right amount of time to every project and every relationship.

Disciplining or Punishing

We saw from the *Andy Griffith* episode how one person (all right, a fictitious one) showed ethical intelligence in the difficult art of discipline. The next time you're in a position to discipline or punish someone, demonstrate ethical intelligence by your willingness to be fair rather than being swayed by things that shouldn't matter. One of the questions on the quiz in chapter 1 concerned an errant employee who is the daughter of a friend of yours. Should your friendship determine how you deal with the problem? It does for many people, but it shouldn't, as I'll discuss when we review the quiz. Lots of things can influence the way you discipline someone — company policies, the law, what's going on in your personal life, how you're feeling at the moment — but disciplining someone in an ethically intelligent way means putting aside everything that isn't relevant, as hard as that may be.[14]

Rectifying Injustice

I recall reading in *Backstreets* magazine many years ago that when Bruce Springsteen was a boy, he was walking down the street in his hometown when he ran into some older kids, one of whom spit on him. Springsteen said that he felt humiliated, and rightly so; no one deserves to be treated like that. This incident may have been a signature moment in his development as a musical artist who strives to inspire his audiences and bring out the best in them. I'm not suggesting that a single nasty episode in Springsteen's life instantly turned him into a person of conscience. But as Springsteen himself noted, being on the receiving end of an injustice stayed with him for years, and it doubtless played a role in the kind of writer and performer he became.

Even those of us who aren't rock stars can rectify injustices when we have the opportunity to do so. Ethical intelligence calls for it. For example, the ethically intelligent manager doesn't stand for injustices such as racial or sexual harassment in the workplace. Yes, this behavior is illegal, but it was wrong even before there were laws against it. It's not just managers, of course, who are in a position to rectify injustices on the job. In 1968, for example, a group of women in England fought to gain equitable treatment of women in the automobile industry. Nigel Cole's film *Made in Dagenham* (written by William Ivory) dramatized their struggle, and it was news to many, including me, that there were no laws anywhere at that time that guaranteed equal pay for equal work. The story of these brave women shows that the courage to challenge the status quo is integrally linked to the ethical responsibility to turn an unjust situation into a just one.

Fairness and the Lemon Problem

The saying "When life gives you lemons, make lemonade" can prompt you to make the best of a bad situation. But suppose you're on the receiving end of a serious injustice, such as discrimination based on age, gender, disability, or race? It's one thing to look on the bright side if you've been stood up on a blind date; but being passed over for a job because you're sixty-two, female, disabled, or African American is a more serious injustice and thus calls for a different approach.

Or does it? When you've been treated wrongly and the stakes are high, it is possible — and indeed essential — to respond with ethical intelligence. You can allow the situation to get the best of you, and you can strike out in vengeance; or you can take action that honors your inherent dignity. This isn't to say it's possible to single-handedly vanquish systemic injustices such as racism or sexism, or that it's wrong to allow yourself to experience unpleasant, even harsh, emotions after you've been treated unfairly. However, the ethically intelligent way to handle any sort of injustice, wherever you find it and in whatever form it takes, is this:

- *Realize* that the other party is to blame, not you.
- *Refuse* to allow the situation to get the best of you. Let reason temper your rage.
- *Respond* in a way that brings out the best in you.

Faced with job discrimination, for example, you could hire an attorney and seek legal redress, but a better use of your time, energy, and money might be finding an employer who values what you bring to the table.[15]

We've now looked at four principles that are the basis of ethical intelligence. But there is one more principle that ethically intelligent people live by. It may be the most important one of all.

PRINCIPLE 5: BE LOVING

You might be surprised to find this principle presented as an element of ethical intelligence. Discussions about ethics usually center around issues raised by the first four principles. As Tina Turner might ask, "What's love got to do with it?" Here's how I'd respond to the Queen of Rock and Roll.

Recently, I purchased a scaled-down version of a stair-climbing machine to use for workouts in my apartment when it's too cold to go for a run outside. For the first few days, the device worked smoothly, but then it developed an annoying squeak. It still functioned adequately, but using it became a much less pleasant experience than it had been, because of the noise. After doing some research on the Internet, I discovered that the favored solution was squirting a bit of WD-40 on the moving parts, and sure enough, the problem disappeared after I did this. Now, not only did the machine work well; it was more agreeable to use.

Love is like the WD-40 of relationships: it's not absolutely necessary, and you couldn't be blamed for not using it — but it sure does make things flow better. Applying the first four principles of ethical intelligence is much easier to do when you use a little bit of love.

If love seems hard to fathom in a business context, just think of care, compassion, or kindness instead. They're close cousins.

Love Is a Many-Splendored (and Many-Faceted) Thing

The word *love* is usually used in one of the following contexts:

- "I love my children."
- "I love my sweetheart."
- "I love old movies."
- "I love chocolate."

As powerful as these feelings can be, the concept of love historically didn't apply just to romance, parenting, or the pleasure associated with eating and leisure activities. It was much broader in scope, as Erich Fromm notes in *The Art of Loving*.[16] Smiling at the people you pass on the street, saying "thank you" to the cashier at the grocery store, or truly listening during a conversation rather than thinking about the next thing you're going to say are all loving things to do. Love in this sense is what some call "brotherly love" and is akin to care or compassion. It is the basis of the fifth and final principle of ethical intelligence.

In his book *How to Win Friends and Influence People*, Dale Carnegie talks about the importance of showing sincere appreciation to the people in your life.[17] Although Carnegie's book is sometimes thought of as a tool for salespeople to increase their ability to close deals, the rules Carnegie presents make a lot of sense for anyone who wants to have strong, meaningful connections to people.

Consider Carnegie's suggestion to give honest and sincere appreciation. You don't have to be in sales to recognize the importance of letting people know when they're doing a good job. They feel good for being recognized for their hard work, and you feel good for making their day. Employees who feel appreciated usually do better work, and stick around longer, than those who don't. At the very least, taking an active interest in the people who work for and with you enhances their feelings of well-being, as a recent Gallup Poll has shown.[18]

ARE THE PRINCIPLES OF ETHICAL INTELLIGENCE NECESSARY OR OPTIONAL?

Philosophers use the technical terms *obligatory* and *supererogatory* to refer to two different kinds of actions: those that are required and those that are above and beyond the call of duty. The five principles of ethical intelligence — Do No Harm, Make Things Better, Respect Others, Be Fair, and Be Loving — tell us what we ought to do. But are these calls to action obligatory or something that's nice to practice but not required?

This isn't merely a matter of semantics, because two important things are at stake: the kinds of things you are rightly expected to do and how you should regard people who don't do them. Suppose, for example, that your job description includes landing two new clients a month and that for the past three months, you have done just that. Can you rightly expect praise? No. You did what you were supposed to do. But if next month you land six clients, that is indeed praiseworthy. Of course, it still behooves your supervisor to express his appreciation to you from time to time, even if you're just doing your job, but if you don't receive such accolades, you can hardly claim to have been slighted. You are, though, entitled to praise if you go above and beyond what you've agreed to do.

It isn't praiseworthy to avoid harming people, as the first principle of ethical intelligence exhorts us to do. It's the least that can be expected. Making things better, as the second principle specifies, may not be a legal requirement, but ethically intelligent people do it anyway. Some use a theological justification by appealing to the commandments of their religious traditions; others hold that using our abilities to make a positive difference in the world is what gives life meaning. Either way, we opt out of this at our peril.

Keeping private things private, telling the truth, and honoring the promises we make — all of which are elements of the third principle of ethical intelligence, Respect Others — are also not above and beyond the call of duty. They are the foundation of our relationships. And when we put the fourth principle, Be Fair, into practice by disciplining someone appropriately, we can't expect a pat on the back for doing so. This is simply what an ethically intelligent person does.

It's when we get to the fifth principle of ethical intelligence, Be Loving, that it may not make sense to speak of obligations or requirements. Can you rightly be faulted for not being compassionate toward the guy yelling into his cell phone in front of you at Starbucks, or the driver who cuts you off on the highway and then curses at you, or the neighbor who refuses to turn her music down? I don't think so. It might be good for both you and them if you can find a way to be loving toward these obnoxious individuals, but expecting you to be compassionate toward them is asking too much. For the people closest to you, then yes, the fifth principle can't be set aside without good reason. For the encounters you have with the rest of the world, only the first four principles of ethical intelligence are essential.

Choosing not to do caring or compassionate things may not amount to an ethical violation, but it's not consistent with ethical intelligence, either. The ethically intelligent person goes above and beyond the call of duty when possible (depending on the circumstances), even though, strictly speaking, he or she isn't ethically required to do so. To be an ethically intelligent person is to strive to be the best human being one can be. There are many benefits to living this way — peace of mind, strong and meaningful relationships, a feeling of purpose and direction — but it's also worth remembering that the main reason to live an ethically intelligent life is because it's the right thing to do.

ARE THERE SHARP DISTINCTIONS AMONG THE PRINCIPLES?

To say that there are five principles (or five anything) is to imply that each member of the group is unique and distinct from the others. But there is some inevitable overlap among the five principles. For example, when you write a note to a friend who has lost a family member, your compassionate act will probably make things a little bit better for your friend. It thus honors both the second and the fifth principles of ethical intelligence. Making things better for someone avoids harming that person, so the first principle of ethical intelligence is upheld, too.

The list of five principles is intended to delineate our responsibilities toward one another (or, in the case of the fifth principle, an ideal to which we should aspire). The principles are broad in scope and cover a lot of ground, so it's not surprising that they intersect in places. They shouldn't be thought of as constituting a checklist or providing a formula for doing the right thing. It's better to regard them as a framework for making ethically intelligent choices in every area of your life. In their simplicity, they offer a way for you to think through tough problems and arrive at the best possible solutions.

Now that we've taken a closer look at the five principles of ethical intelligence, the next chapter will show how they apply to the quiz presented in chapter 1.

SUMMARY

The first principle of ethical intelligence, Do No Harm, is a principle of nonintervention. We apply it by restraining the impulse to do or say harmful things. However, two corollaries call upon us to do something, rather than nothing:

- Prevent Harm
- Minimize Unavoidable Harm

The second principle of ethical intelligence, Make Things Better, takes us further and exhorts us to improve the lot of others and ourselves. This underscores how ethics concerns our responsibilities to ourselves and not just to our employer, colleagues, family, and friends.

The third principle of ethical intelligence, Respect Others, has three components:

- Protecting confidentiality
- Telling the truth
- Honoring your promises

The fourth principle of ethical intelligence, Be Fair, means giving others their due. We do this in three critical areas:

- Allocating scarce resources
- Disciplining or punishing others
- Rectifying injustices

The fifth principle of ethical intelligence, Be Loving, speaks not to romantic feelings but to kindness, care, and compassion. It may rightly be understood not as an ethical requirement, as the first four principles are, but rather as an ideal to which we should aspire.

CHAPTER 3

Revisiting the Quiz
What's Your Ethics IQ?

Now that you've learned about the five principles of ethical intelligence, you're in a position to evaluate your responses to the quiz questions from chapter 1 and discover how ethically intelligent you are. Here are the quiz questions again, this time with the most ethically intelligent response indicated for each one.

1. You notice that your friend Heather has posted a new picture of herself on Facebook in which she is smoking a bong with one hand and holding a bottle of vodka in the other. What would you do?

   A. Tell her you don't think this photo is a good idea.
   B. Don't say anything about it to her.
   C. "Like" the photo.
   D. Copy the photo to your hard drive and use it against her if she ever double-crosses you.

The ethically intelligent response is A.

Heather's photo risks violating the first principle of ethical intelligence, Do No Harm, in several ways, and the harm it causes is primarily to Heather herself. First, she could lose her job, or fail to get a raise or promotion, if her employer comes across it. Second, future employers or those who might have other opportunities in store for Heather (grant-making foundations, competitions, volunteer organizations) might choose not to bring Heather into the fold if this image were to come to light. Third, if her employer is identified in her profile, the organization's reputation could be compromised, which is bad for its own sake and bad for what might happen to Heather later.

This isn't the stuff of fantasy. Olympic gold medalist Michael Phelps was photographed smoking a bong and promptly lost a lucrative endorsement deal from Kellogg.[1] Anthony Weiner resigned from the U.S. House of Representatives after sexually suggestive photos he had sent privately through Twitter became public.

Two features of Internet communication are worth noting: its worldwide reach and its permanence. Presumably, Heather wouldn't think of opening her bedroom window and yelling, "I'm smoking pot now!" But if she did, maybe ten or twelve people in her neighborhood would hear her. The Facebook picture, however, is visible to potentially the entire world. Even if her privacy setting is set to "viewable by friends only," all one friend has to do is download it and post it elsewhere. Whatever you post, you're essentially putting on a billboard large enough to be seen around the globe.

Remember the James Bond film *Diamonds Are Forever*? It's not just precious jewels that are forever; everything on the Internet is, too. Every email you've ever sent, every tweet you've ever tweeted, and every Facebook post you've ever made are capable of being excavated, and it's almost impossible to erase what you've tossed into cyberspace.[2] The ethically intelligent person keeps this in mind before hitting Send on his or her computer keyboard.

The Prevent Harm corollary of the first principle of ethical intelligence calls upon you to let Heather know that she should seriously consider removing the photo from her Facebook page. It is all the more incumbent upon you to do so because Heather is a friend of yours. She may balk at this suggestion, but if you let her know about the potentially harmful consequences to her career and her reputation that the photo poses, your argument could be persuasive. Even if she laughs it off now, she could very well reconsider the matter later on, especially if other friends like you reinforce the message. She could also choose to keep the photo posted. There is only so much you can do to protect Heather from a harm that she can't or won't recognize. However, being someone's friend means making a good faith effort to help that friend correct a mistake that could come back to haunt him or her. The sooner Heather takes the photo off Facebook, the better her chances are of avoiding harm to herself and, if she has identified her employer in her profile, to the company she works for.

2. You're having lunch at a restaurant and overhear two colleagues, Bob and Ray, talking about a client with whom your business is having difficulty. They mention the client by name as well as specific information about the problem. What would you do?

   A. Approach them and mention your concerns about confidentiality.
   B. Ignore it.
   C. Tell your supervisor what you witnessed.
   D. Record your colleagues with your cell phone's video camera and post the clip on YouTube.

The ethically intelligent response is A.

Most likely Bob and Ray are being negligent rather than intentionally malicious. They're simply not thinking about the potential consequences of what they're doing. But those consequences can be quite severe; if people in the vicinity overhear the conversation and pass the information along, it can get twisted and end up hurting someone who isn't even involved in the matter. But even if that information is passed along with 100 percent accuracy, it belongs to the client. He or she has trusted your colleagues (and, by implication, the entire company) to keep private things private. Recall that the third principle of ethical intelligence, Respect Others, requires doing just this. Even if Bob and Ray mean no harm by what they're doing, and even if no one overhears Bob and Ray's conversation, they're still taking something that has been entrusted to them and isn't theirs, and treating it disrespectfully.

Bob and Ray's public conversation is not consistent with ethical intelligence. I'm not saying that Bob and Ray are bad people but rather that their actions are not compatible with this book's main idea. What does any of this have to do with you? By being an eyewitness — or more accurately, an earwitness — you are called to action. You are, after all, in a position to protect client confidentiality (thereby upholding principle 3, Respect Others) and to prevent harm to others (which honors principle 1, Do No Harm). The potential harm here is both to your company (since what Bob and Ray are doing tarnishes its reputation for respecting its clients and could result in lost business) and to the client (because of what Bob and Ray may be revealing in their conversation).

The ethically intelligent thing to do is to talk with your colleagues about your concerns. You'd want to do this privately, lest you undercut the very principles you're trying to uphold. You might want to use the "praise sandwich" technique of giving criticism:

1. *Begin with something sincere and pleasing.* You could start by saying, "Hey, Bob and Ray! It's always good to see you." This will make it more likely that they will take to heart the next thing you're going to say.

2. *Focus on what you observed.* For example, you could say, "You know, I couldn't help but overhear you talking about a client, and if I could hear it, maybe other people in the restaurant could, too."

3. *Expect the best from them.* You might say something like

this: "I'm sure you weren't aware of what you were doing, because I know both of you, and you're good guys."

How you give unpleasant news usually determines how it will
be taken. The kind but firm admonition of the praise sandwich
all but guarantees your concerns will be taken seriously, and that
will be the end of the matter.

In the unlikely event that Bob or Ray, or both, tell you to get
lost or promise to be careful but do the same thing again, you not
only have a right to notify their supervisor but you have an ethical
obligation to do so. But the ethically intelligent thing to do first is to
muster the courage to have an open and honest talk with Bob and
Ray and leave it at that.

Note that this analysis assumes your organization does not
require you to report confidentiality violations immediately. During a workshop I gave to members of the South Carolina National
Guard, where I presented this scenario, a guardsman said, "Sir, we
have to tell our commanding officer what we witnessed. It's in our
regulations, and we could be dismissed if we don't honor them." In
such a case, the ethically intelligent course is different from the one
described above, where there is no such policy in place.

3. You take your twelve-year-old son to the movies. At the box
   office, you see a sign that says, "Children up to eleven: $6.00.
   Adults: $12.00." The movie theater's management thus consid-
   ers your son to be an adult. What would you do?

   A. Ask for one adult's and one child's ticket.
   B. Ask for two adult's tickets.
   C. Give your son the money and have him ask for a ticket.
   D. Ask your son what he thinks you should do, and then do
      whatever he suggests.

The ethically intelligent response is B.

Business ethics is usually presented as a subject that concerns what businesses owe to consumers, such as safe products, fair return policies, and a truthful account of the goods or services that are for sale. But business ethics also concerns how customers treat businesses. In this example, the movie theater has decided to offer a discount to children, and it has chosen eleven years old as the cutoff point for determining who counts as a child. It's true that the line is arbitrarily drawn; some theaters draw it at twelve years old, and some at thirteen years old. Still others offer no discount at all, and they're entitled to do this. Why? Because we don't have a right to a discount at the movies. The theater in question wants to make it affordable for families to take their kids to a film, and their discount policy for kids up to eleven is reasonable. Since your twelve-year-old son isn't a child from the theater's perspective, the right thing to do — the ethically intelligent thing to do — is to buy two adult's tickets. In doing so, you're showing your son that although he could pass as an eleven-year-old, it's not right to take advantage of the theater's naïveté. Even if you plan to give the money you save back to the theater at the concession stand, you're still violating the business's policy. The fourth principle of ethical intelligence, Be Fair, calls upon us to give others their due, and honoring a reasonable policy is consistent with this.

Of course, just because a business has a policy in place doesn't mean that the policy should automatically command our respect. Some movie theaters used to have a "whites only" policy. But, of course, this was wrong, and it didn't deserve to be honored.

4. An employee you supervise comes to work late, spends a lot of time shopping online, takes long lunches and coffee breaks, and leaves early. A few months ago, you fired someone for doing the same thing. This person, however, is the daughter of a close

personal friend. You've talked with her several times about her conduct, but the problems continue. What would you do?

A. Fire her.
B. Ignore it.
C. Talk with her again and tell her this is her last chance to straighten up.
D. Ask your friend (her parent) to talk with her.

The ethically intelligent response is A.

The fourth principle of ethical intelligence, Be Fair, tells us to give others their due, and as we have discussed, the way you punish or discipline people reveals how fair you are. What is the appropriate punishment for a slacker whose father is a friend of yours?

You have already established the right precedent for handling errant employees who continue to shirk their responsibilities: you let them go. After all, when employees accept their job offers, they're essentially making a promise to do what is expected of them. The employer makes a promise in return: to pay the employee and perhaps to offer sick days, paid vacation, and health insurance. If either side reneges, the deal is off. If your company is no longer able to pay its employees, it's hardly fair to expect them to continue working. By the same token, it's not fair to the other employees who fulfill their job descriptions to keep a slacker on the payroll. The employment contract isn't merely a legal arrangement; it's an ethical one, too.

Since you have a precedent, you're in a good position to decide the ethically intelligent response to the above situation. "Treat like cases alike, and unalike cases unalike," a rule that has its roots in Aristotle's *Nicomachean Ethics*,[3] is a good guideline to follow. The only significant difference between the precedent and the current situation is that you have a personal connection to this employee, and you didn't with the previous one. But this fact isn't ethically relevant. Presumably, the policy at your business isn't "Fire unproductive employees, unless you're friends with their parents." The friendship might *feel* like something you should take into account, since you might anger your friend by letting his daughter go, but the friendship has no connection to your company or its mission. Asking your friend to get involved is thus not appropriate. You're fobbing off your professional responsibility onto someone else.

Giving the employee yet another chance to get her act together is merely biding time. It's an understandable impulse, perhaps, but it's not ethically intelligent. Besides, if you kept her on, how do you think this would affect office morale? Other employees would rightly feel that you're playing favorites — because you would be.

The fair response, and thus the ethically intelligent one, is to let her go. But what happens if your friend really does get angry with you and puts your friendship on the line? Your response should be to stand your ground. A true friend wouldn't expect you to violate your ethical responsibilities, and there is no good ethical reason for keeping the loafer on board. If your so-called friend decides to end the friendship, it will be unpleasant, it will hurt, but *it will not be your problem*!

The way you handle this situation will reveal how committed to the principle of fairness — and thus ethical intelligence — you are as a manager.

5. You wake up on a workday with the flu. What would you do?

    A. Stay at home and rest.

    B. Stay at home and work.

    C. Go to work but avoid socializing with people.

    D. Go to work but socialize only with the people you don't like.

The ethically intelligent response is A.

The flu is contagious and potentially deadly. The first corollary to the Do No Harm principle, Prevent Harm, points in the direction of staying home. The fifth principle of ethical intelligence, Be Loving, takes it a step further: doing work at home would be unkind to yourself and would make it take longer for you to get better. Staying at home and resting is thus the ethically intelligent response to this common problem. Loyalty to one's company and the desire to avoid being a burden to one's coworkers are noble impulses, but you'll do more harm than good by going to work sick. Everyone, including you, will be better off if you take a few days or even longer to restore your health.

YOUR ETHICS IQ

Now that you've seen how the five principles of ethical intelligence apply in the scenarios from the quiz, it's time to find out how ethically intelligent you are. If you selected the ethically intelligent choice:

- 0–1 time, your grade is F
- 2 times, your grade is D
- 3 times, your grade is C
- 4 times, your grade is B
- 5 times, your grade is A

If your grade is D or F, then you've come to the right place for help! It appears that you are more likely to do what's easy than what's right. If you're willing to take the ideas in this book to heart, however, you may just find that not only will other people be better off — you will be, too.

If your grade is B or C, then you suffer from Charlie Brown syndrome: wishy-washiness. Sometimes you take the high road, and sometimes you don't. The ethically intelligent path can be hard to follow; yet in the long run, it's the right way to go, as you'll see throughout the rest of this book.

If your grade is A, then you are a model human being! Nevertheless, there's always room for improvement, so I hope you'll continue reading. Doing so may help you stay on track and continue being such an ethically intelligent person.

SUMMARY

How you responded to these scenarios in this chapter reveals how ethically intelligent you are.

A Facebook Friend's Photo

When a friend posts an incriminating picture of herself on Facebook, the duty to prevent harm calls upon you to encourage her to remove the photo and to explain why it is in her own interest to do so.

Colleagues with Loose Lips

When you observe colleagues violating client confidentiality (which compromises your client's right to privacy as well as the reputation of your company), you ought to share your concerns privately with your co-workers. The drastic step of reporting your colleagues is usually not necessary unless your organization requires you to do so.

The Box Office Dilemma

Customers should abide by the fair policies that businesses create, such as a movie theater's requirement that children over a certain age to pay full price for admission.

A Friend's Daughter at Work

If you have previously fired employees for slacking off, the fourth principle of ethical intelligence, Be Fair, calls for you to do the same for an employee who is doing that now, even if she happens to be the daughter of a friend of yours.

Waking Up Sick

It is ethically unintelligent to go to work when you have the flu, because doing so violates the Do No Harm and Be Loving principles.

CHAPTER 4

Ten Questions about Ethics and Ethical Intelligence

O ur exploration of ethical intelligence thus far has probably raised a few questions for you. Here are answers to the ten questions that people who have attended my presentations ask me most frequently.

1. Is there a difference between morality and ethics?

Not historically. In fact, the word "morality" comes from *moralis*, a Latin word that Cicero coined as a translation of the Greek word *ethikos*, which is the origin of the term "ethics." Thus "morality" is to "ethics" what *chapeau* is to "hat" or *caliente* is to "hot."

It's true that many, perhaps most, people make a distinction between morality and ethics, but the problem is that no two people seem to agree about what that distinction is. Test this claim by asking five people you know, "Do you believe there is a difference between ethics and morality? If so, what is that difference?" You'll get responses like these:

- Ethics has to do with social standards; morality is about personal beliefs.
- Ethics comes from secular institutions, whereas morality is a religious phenomenon.

- Ethical judgments are absolute and objective; moral judgments are relative and subjective.

Not only do folks differ about what the distinction between the concepts is; they also differ about how to define each one. Even those who believe there is no difference between ethics and morality may differ over how to define them.

Yow! This sure is confusing. But it doesn't have to be, because just about everyone understands that *both* ethics and morality have to do with identifying right conduct and good character. To keep everyone on the same page, and to honor the linguistic history of these two concepts, it's much better to treat *ethical* and *moral* as synonymous.

In this book (and in all of my writing and public speaking), I avoid using the word *moral*, because it makes some people see red when I interchange that word with *ethical*. I'd rather focus on what's really important — discovering the best ways to respond to difficult situations and understanding why those approaches are right. This is, I suspect, why you're reading this book in the first place.

2. Why don't more people do the right thing? What gets in the way?

Explaining the reasons why it's hard to consistently do the right thing would require a book of its own (and probably more than one). Nevertheless, there are three major explanations for ethically unintelligent behavior, and they're easy to remember because they all start — and appropriately so — with *f*: fear, focus on short-term benefits, and foul mood. Let's look at each one more closely.

1. *Fear.* At the root of peer pressure is fear: the fear of not being cool. Young people are especially susceptible to this type of fear since kids and adolescents value approval so much. It still bothers me that I stole a pocket-sized can of breath spray from a pharmacy

when I was ten simply because a friend urged me to do it. I knew it was wrong, but I did it anyway.

But fear gives rise to a lot of unethical behavior among adults, too. When you know your boss has a drinking problem, you may fear reprisals if you intervene in some way (by contacting your organization's employee assistance program, for example). Even if your company has a policy that prohibits retaliation, you might decide to do nothing about the problem because you don't want your boss to be angry with you in the event that the boss finds out it was you who intervened. We all want to be on good terms with our supervisors, but the lengths to which we go to achieve this can be at odds with ethical intelligence.

2. *Focus on short-term benefits.* As someone who struggles constantly with weight, I know all too well how tempting those vanilla cupcakes with chocolate buttercream frosting from Magnolia Bakery can be. I also know that if I eat one and I'm not willing to work out for an extra hour to burn it off, then I'll pay a price. But, heck, it looks *so* good — why not indulge now and worry about the results later? Placing a greater priority on immediate benefits (in this case, intense gustatory pleasure) than on long-term benefits (such as maintaining a healthy weight) is a problem that can crop up in many contexts — not just when it comes to deciding whether to wolf down a tasty morsel but also when it comes to matters of far greater importance, such as how to do business.

For example, some businesses outsource their customer service positions because overseas jobs cost less, which means profits will be greater. However, companies that engage in this practice can generate so much ill will among their customers, who are frustrated with being unable to communicate effectively with their "customer care associates," that in the long run, these businesses may lose the very people they claim to be serving. (I'll look at this issue in more detail in chapter 8.) Yes, the marketplace is increasingly crowded, and the pressure to be profitable is greater than ever. But businesses that keep customer service jobs at home are both ethically intelligent and more likely to remain profitable far beyond the next several quarters.

3. *Foul mood.* It's hard to treat others with loving-kindness when you haven't had enough sleep, you've just gotten some bad news, or you're having problems with a relationship. When you're feeling bad, it's more difficult to restrain the impulse to be nasty or even hurtful. You know that person in your life who knows exactly what it takes to push your buttons and does so at every opportunity? It's their own emotional issues, rather than anything you've said or done, that's most likely at the heart of this antisocial behavior.

Make no mistake: I'm merely trying to explain, not justify, why it's sometimes challenging to live according to the five principles of ethical intelligence. But if you're aware of the things that are likely to trip you up, you can be on guard against them and improve the odds of making ethically intelligent choices. Understanding a problem is the first step toward fixing it and preventing it from recurring.

3. In chapter 1, you say that the five principles of ethical intelligence are "the bedrock of Eastern and Western religious traditions alike." Yet not only do different religions often have different views about what is right and wrong, but there is also a lot of argument within each faith about what constitutes right and wrong. Furthermore, there doesn't appear to be a consensus across cultures about ethics. How do you account for these differences?

There are certainly plenty of examples of differences across religions and cultures when it comes to issues directly or tangentially related to ethics. Jews and Muslims believe that it is wrong to eat pork, but this isn't true for many Christians; Jains are required to abstain from eating animals altogether. For Christians and Hindus, human beings have souls, but Buddhists reject this idea (at least in the way the term *soul* is commonly understood). These differences aren't trivial, and they can and do give rise to heated discussions across the traditions, as well as within each one. Is it right for Jewish women to become rabbis (scholars qualified to rule on Jewish law)? In Orthodox Judaism, the answer is no; in Reform Judaism, it is yes. Catholics believe it is permissible and even obligatory to receive a blood transfusion if this will save a human life; Jehovah's Witnesses hold that it is wrong to do so. There has never been, and there probably will never be, universal agreement among religious traditions about precisely how human beings ought to live.

But the above examples merely show that followers of religious traditions, and the texts upon which their religions are based, have different interpretations of how ethical principles apply in particular instances. The same is true with respect to cultures. Every faith or social group that has ever existed, or is likely to exist, calls upon its members to follow the five principles of ethical intelligence: Do No Harm, Make Things Better, Respect Others, Be Fair, and Be Loving. Not all groups codify these principles into law, nor do they all agree on what it means to be respectful or fair, or even on what constitutes harm. It's also true that history is filled with atrocities committed in the name of God. But the problem is not the religions themselves or their commitment to ethical behavior but the misguided faithful who twist the peaceful messages to meet their own objectives. If you and your friend play Scrabble online and your friend cheats by consulting a Scrabble website, where does the fault lie — with the rules of Scrabble or with your friend?

At their most fundamental and meaningful level — the level of principle — religions and cultures alike are committed to the same ethical ideas and ideals. Misguided members of religious communities, and even those who are conscientious, may make ethical blunders, but this doesn't detract from the integrity of the sacred texts themselves and the ethical principles upon which they are founded.

4. Slavery used to be a widespread, and even legally sanctioned, practice in the United States, and now it isn't. Even today, some cultures allow practices that strike others as horrific and deeply unethical. What does it matter that there is agreement at the level of ethical principles if there are discrepancies where it counts the most — how people actually treat one another?

Just because a practice is widely accepted doesn't mean that it is acceptable. Slavery in the United States before the Civil War is a good example of this; the fact that many white people had slaves didn't mean that it was right, even if there were no legal proscriptions against doing so. What changed after the war wasn't the rightness or wrongness of the practice of slavery but the views of those who, for a variety of reasons, came to recognize that slavery is wrong.

It's also worth considering how it is that a practice such as slavery (or foot binding, or female genital mutilation, or any other severe violation of human dignity) comes to be accepted in the first place. This "acceptance" is often the result of one group of people abusing their power over another group rather than the result of a rational discussion among equals. If the people on the receiving end of the injustice are denied a voice, how can such a practice ever be considered legitimate?

5. What's the difference between ethics and the law?

When we ask, "What is the right thing to do?" we're asking an ethical question. Sometimes laws are relevant to answering this question, and sometimes they are not. For example, if you want to know whether it's right to withhold or withdraw life-sustaining medical treatment from an elderly aunt who is irreversibly ill, it's worth knowing that the medical power of attorney that she signed authorizing this is legally binding. But if you want to know whether you should tell a close friend that his wife is cheating on him, there are no applicable laws to speak of, and it's a good thing that this is the case. Few people would want the state to have authority over such personal matters.

However, it still makes sense to ask about any law, "Is it right?" Regarding the first example above, laws that require advance directives to be respected are based on the ethical principle of respect for patient autonomy. Even before the law compelled family members and health-care providers to respect the wishes of patients who wanted to stop end-of-life care, patients were entitled to have their wishes respected, and thus others had an obligation to do so. Of course, it was the law that gave this obligation teeth. There is nothing like the force of law to encourage people to do the right thing.

There have been, and continue to be, bad laws, and from an ethical perspective, such laws do not command respect. In some parts of the country, African Americans were legally required to use separate water fountains, go to the balcony of movie theaters (if they were allowed in at all), and sit at the rear of public buses. These laws were unjust; so in 1955 when Rosa Parks refused to give up her bus seat to a white man in Montgomery, Alabama, she broke the law, but she did the right thing. But she also paid a price for her civil disobedience, namely, going to jail and receiving death threats. Those who choose to disregard laws they consider unjust must also be willing to accept the consequences of doing so.

Laws are an essential component of civilized society. But laws are sometimes wrong. So when you ask yourself, "What should I do?" your reflection should — where appropriate — include a consideration of the law but shouldn't end there.

6. What made you an authority on what everyone else should do?

Ethicists run the risk of being seen as self-righteous. After all, much of what we do involves making judgments about what's right and wrong. But being an ethicist isn't merely about making such evaluations; it's also about justifying those claims — that is, constructing arguments for or against certain positions. Conversations in which people express how they feel about the issues of the day can be fun and lively, but ethics seeks to rise above merely stating one's strongly held opinions and to establish truth, or a close approximation thereof.

It is this notion of "rising above" that opens us ethicists up to charges of feeling superior to others. Can there really be *experts* in ethics? The idea of ethical expertise intrigued me so much that I made it the basis of my doctoral dissertation, in which I explained what ethics experts are and what they are not.[1] I can't claim to be better than you, but I can say that the project I've put forth here, and the arguments I'm making about a wide range of ethical issues, are the result of extensive training in, reflection on, and teaching about these very matters.

Ethicists seek to provide a rational basis for ethical judgments, and it is the ability to do so that distinguishes our work and makes it worth taking seriously. This is because a statement is more likely to be true if it is supported by a good argument. However, ethicists are human beings and are subject to the same sort of temptations, weaknesses, and frailties that everyone else is. Thus, even if I'm able to provide good reasons for not doing x and I know that I shouldn't do it, it's still possible that one will end up doing it anyway.

Ethics is a democratic field, and anyone can and should challenge the claims that ethicists make. Not only *can* you look critically at everything I say in this book; it would be irresponsible if you did not. For example, if I'm correct in concluding that ethically intelligent businesses do not outsource customer service, it's because I've provided a valid argument to support this claim, not because it's The Ethics Guy saying so. The ethically intelligent life is a rational one, and this means carefully considering the judgments that others make and the arguments they use to support those judgments. Nowhere is this responsibility more crucial than in the field concerned with how best to live your life: ethics.

7. What do you mean by the term *intelligence?*

Intelligence includes both a capacity to be, and a state of being, smart. In fact, the second entails the first, since one can be smart only if one is capable of being smart in the first place.

But it is wrong to think that intelligence is concerned merely with the intellect. It's true that *intelligence* and *intellect* have a common root, but intelligence is just as much about *doing* as it is about *being*. After all, the intelligent person does intelligent things (not always, but more often than not).

8. Isn't it elitist to link smartness or intelligence with ethics? This suggests that only educated people can do the right thing or even know what that is.

The concept of ethical intelligence should not be seen as elitist and is in fact its polar opposite: populist. Some people become smart through formal education, and others do so through experience. But neither education nor experience guarantees that a person will develop intelligence. Even if one has the capacity to become an intelligent person, a degree from a top school may simply indicate a skill at doing what the school requires to graduate (such as attending classes, achieving passing grades, and the like). There are more than a few unintelligent people with advanced degrees.

Similarly, the fact that a person has had a wide range of experiences doesn't mean that he or she has learned from those experiences and is now a wise person.

Ethical intelligence is a populist idea because just about everyone can live in an ethically intelligent way. As I'll show in the forthcoming chapters, ethical intelligence, however one goes about possessing it, is an essential component to living well.

9. Can ethical intelligence be learned?

Yes, and we already have a head start. After all, we learned the five principles of ethics from our parents and teachers. But it's easy to put these principles aside when it's convenient or to convince ourselves that ethical principles are no longer important. Even when we're committed to doing the right thing, it isn't always apparent what the right thing is. For example, outsourcing customer service overseas will save your company money, but is this practice ethically intelligent? A quick review of the five principles doesn't present an obvious answer, but a thoughtful analysis of how the principles apply to this issue does provide guidance, as I'll show in chapter 8.

You weren't born knowing how to act; you discovered it through reflection and experience.

10. So, in a nutshell, what is ethical intelligence?

Ethical intelligence has three components:

1. The capacity to discover the right course of action
2. Acting upon what you discover
3. The commitment to making this exploration a lifelong journey

SUMMARY

The examination of ten frequently asked questions about ethics and ethical intelligence yields the following insights:

- There is no meaningful distinction between ethics and morality. *Ethical* and *moral* can and should be used interchangeably.

- Fear, focus on short-term benefits, and foul moods can make it difficult to do the right thing.

- Differences in social practices exist across religions, but Eastern and Western religions alike are founded on the ethical concepts represented by the five principles of ethical intelligence.

- An action can be ethical but illegal, or unethical but legally permissible (or even legally required). For any law, we can and should ask, "Is the law right?"

- Experts in ethics can't legitimately claim to be better people, but their training and experience may make them well suited to evaluate the rightness or wrongness of what people do.

- Ethical intelligence is a populist idea, not an elitist one, and it can be developed and strengthened through both reflection and practice.

PART 2

Ethical Intelligence at Work

CHAPTER 5

Plays Well with Others
Ethical Intelligence
with the People Who Work *with* You

You're only as strong as the people who work with you. In this chapter, we'll look at ethically intelligent ways of dealing with coworkers. We'll focus on three issues:

- Office romances
- Talking politics on the job
- Dealing with people you can't stand

LOOKING FOR LOVE IN ALL THE WRONG PLACES: · OFFICE ROMANCES

When David Letterman admitted that he'd had sex with several of the women who worked for him, the national discussion about dating in the workplace that had been simmering for years finally exploded. Is it right to date a coworker? Your boss? Someone who works for you? Let's consider whether office romances are consistent with ethical intelligence.

The Truth about Dating

Most romantic relationships don't work out. Think about it: How many people do you know who are still in a relationship with the first person they ever dated? It's a good thing that this is the case. After all, it takes time to find the right person. But what does "the right person" mean, anyway?

I remember a conversation I had as a young professor with my boss at the time. We were driving back from a workshop we'd given and were having a heart-to-heart conversation about marriage, since I was single then.

"Bruce, what do you think makes a relationship work?" he asked.

"Shared interests," I said. "Mutual attraction."

"Those are important," he replied, "but shared values are what really matter."

His words have stayed with me because I think he's right. There's no doubt that physical attraction jump-starts a relationship. Once that relationship gets going, it's great to discover that both you and the other person love sports, traveling, or the films of Alfred Hitchcock. But what takes the relationship from a sprint to a marathon is a shared commitment to the things that matter most. That is, shared values. And values are revealed over time by how the person acts, not by what he or she says.

Since it takes time to get to know a person and what his or her values are, the office is the obvious place to look for love or for love to find you. With a fragile economy and increased financial worry, we're spending more time on the job than ever before. Seeing someone every day gives you a good sense of what that person is really like, much more so than a few dates with someone does. The workplace does seem like the best possible arena for finding a lifelong partner.

But the fact that most relationships don't work out is the reason why dating in the workplace is not consistent with ethical intelligence. If, after a few dates with someone you know from outside of work, you discover that you're not interested in pursuing a relationship with that person and you call it quits, you probably won't see him or her again (unless you live in a very small town). If, however, your romantic relationship with a coworker fizzles out, as it almost certainly will, you have to see that person day after day, and that's where the problems begin. I know from personal experience how excruciating it is to sit at your desk stewing with anger, hurt, and bewilderment after you have a falling out with the person down the hall. It's hard to focus on your work, and it becomes difficult to do your job well. You may wind up letting clients down, tarnishing the reputation of the company, and making it more difficult for yourself to move on. Dating a coworker is thus one of the surest ways to violate the first principle of ethical intelligence, Do No Harm.

How Office Morale, Clients, and Your Business Can Be Adversely Affected

A lawyer I know from a major law firm — I'll call her Emily — told me about how an office romance threatened the firm's relationship with a client. The couple in question — I'll call them Jake and Isabelle — were prone to displays of affection around the office. One day, they were smooching after hours in front of a conference room, which they believed was empty. It looked empty from their cursory glance, but one of the firm's clients was in the room and felt uncomfortable enough about what he witnessed to complain to Emily.

What kind of review do you think this client gave the firm to others in his organization? If someone asked him to recommend a good corporate law firm, do you think he would have suggested the one with Jake and Isabelle? If he was moved to bring up the matter then and there, one can only imagine how he spoke about the place to others.

Emily reported the matter to a senior partner, who then confronted Jake and Isabelle. Jake argued that he and Isabelle did their best to be discreet, but they were really in love and felt that their relationship should be respected.

It turns out that the client wasn't the only one who was bothered by Jake and Isabelle's romantic relationship. A lot of the people who worked near them felt uncomfortable as well, and they, too, had notified the senior partner. Nobody begrudged them their happiness, but when you are working hard to earn your pay, there is something disconcerting about knowing your coworkers are spending their work time kissing. When Jake went into Isabelle's office and closed the door, some of their coworkers wondered, "Are they having a business meeting, or are they just making out?" The senior partner ultimately gave Jake and Isabelle thirty days for one or both to leave the firm.

A manager I once had told a few staff members at lunch one day that she and her boyfriend had been having sex all over the office — including on the round table where we were eating! She presented it as something funny, but I was troubled by her decision to sexualize the workplace. There was also the obvious hygienic concern: Who wants to worry about whether the desk they're writing on had a couple of bare bottoms rolling around on it the previous evening?

The first principle of ethical intelligence, Do No Harm, is compromised in several ways by office romances: clients, office morale, and the business's reputation are all at risk.

But there is one other aspect of Jake and Isabelle's relationship worth mentioning: he was her supervisor. Isabelle claimed that she began dating Jake of her own free will and never felt pressured to remain in the relationship for any reason. Perhaps this was so. But, as we will see, dating a subordinate is inconsistent with ethical intelligence.

When Sex and Power Collide

Suppose you're interviewing someone for a new position at work and you find this person quite attractive. I'll assign the name Chris to this candidate to cover both gender possibilities. Several times during the interview, Chris smiles warmly at you, which makes you feel good. As the interview unfolds, you get the feeling that Chris is attracted to you. This is someone you'd love to have on your team. Chris isn't wearing a wedding ring and makes no reference to a boyfriend or girlfriend. You sure would like to hire Chris — but how can you tell that your attraction isn't compromising your ability to assess Chris's abilities accurately? Chris may indeed be the best person for the job, but if one of the reasons that you want this candidate on your team is that you feel a romance is possible, you simply can't be objective.

Let's take it a step further. Others on the interviewing committee believe Chris would be a terrific fit at the company, so Chris is hired. You decide to wait to ask Chris out, just so that you can see whether there is indeed a mutual attraction. You learn that Chris is single. You ask Chris out, but Chris refuses. In fact, Chris appears mortified that you would do such a thing. You explain why. Chris replies, "I'm afraid you've misunderstood me. I'm just a friendly person. I smile a lot. That's the way I am." How will this new development in your relationship affect Chris's work and your relationship with Chris? The outcome may very well be negative for all concerned. You now question whether it was a smart move on your part to hire Chris in the first place. None of this is consistent with ethical intelligence.

But suppose that when you ask Chris out, the answer is yes. How can you be sure that Chris is accepting your invitation out of a genuine interest in you? Chris may be doing so for fear of alienating you, which doesn't bode well for anyone in the long run. Or

Chris may agree to go on the date because Chris's long-term goal is to advance in the company, and this is a sure way to do so. This, too, suggests unpleasant things are in store.

Let's imagine now that Chris has agreed to go out on a date because Chris is indeed attracted to you. The relationship goes great for a while, but ultimately it doesn't work out. Shortly thereafter, the company has to do some downsizing, and you're called upon to do some of this unpleasant work. Chris is one of the people you decide to let go. How can you or Chris know that the unhappy personal relationship wasn't a factor in your decision? You can't, and neither can Chris.

Even if the relationship is genuine and not put to the test of downsizing, there is the issue of appearances. Chris's peers will reasonably wonder if Chris is getting advantages they aren't getting because they're not sleeping with the boss. That's not fair to Chris's peers or to Chris.

Sexual harassment laws were promulgated to prevent just these kinds of nasty situations from occurring and to provide redress when they do. Two forms of sexual harassment exist under the law: the creation of an offensive or hostile environment (which may follow if Chris becomes unwillingly entangled in a romantic relationship with you) and quid pro quo, literally, "something for something" (which could exist if you offer Chris some kind of benefit at work in exchange for sex). Because of its brazen violation of the Do No Harm principle, sexual harassment is obviously inconsistent with ethical intelligence.

But an office romance between a boss and his or her subordinate doesn't have to involve sexual harassment for it to be something that ethically intelligent managers and those who work with them avoid. The waters are simply too perilous to proceed on such a journey. As difficult as it is to "just say no," this is what the ethically intelligent person does when considering whether to date someone at work.

But If You Must...

If, however, two people simply can't resist the call of Cupid, and there is not an imbalance of power between them, ethical intelligence calls for each person to be on a different team at work. Since preventing harm is an important corollary to the first principle of ethical intelligence, smart lovebirds at work, and those who manage them, will ensure that coworkers, clients, the company, and the lovers themselves are not at risk for getting hurt and that the couple's first responsibility on the job — to do their work well — will not be compromised.

I know (and I'll bet you do, too) several couples who met on the job and are now happily married or in a long-term, committed relationship. Two of my professors in college met their wives in class, which seems to provide some evidence against the argument that romantic relationships characterized by an imbalance of power are perilous. Human beings aren't automatons, and as these examples suggest, it is indeed possible to conduct a love affair at work or in school with ethical intelligence.

But the fact that some folks can avoid the pitfalls of an office romance does not mean that this kind of relationship, generally speaking, is smart. In his memoir, *Red: My Uncensored Life in Rock*, Sammy Hagar talks about his love of driving fast on the freeway.[1] He has been pulled over for speeding over forty times and once exceeded 150 miles an hour on Highway 101 in California. Fortunately, his passion for exceeding the speed limit hasn't harmed anyone (yet), but even the man who wrote "I Can't Drive 55" could hardly say that such a policy is a good idea.

Bottom line: Office romances are generally not consistent with ethical intelligence. Dating a coworker may seem to be a great way to apply principle 2, Make Things Better, to one's own life, but this is likely to compromise relationships with coworkers, clients, and the employer. When Freud said that the two essential ingredients for a happy life are work and love, he didn't mean that they're to be found in the same place.

However, if two people at work do fall in love, the ethically intelligent thing to do is for managers to ensure that they don't work together and for the lovebirds themselves to be as discreet as possible.

"I'M RIGHT, AND YOU'RE AN IDIOT!":
TALKING POLITICS AT WORK

Can you think of a time in your life when there was more at stake politically in our country and the world than there is today? Or one that engendered such strong feelings about political issues? Or that featured so many nasty advertisements and personal attacks from candidates for election?

I can't, and I grew up in the 1960s.

With so many troubling issues before us — a fragile economy, tremendous job insecurity, skyrocketing health-care costs — and news about these issues presented in emotionally charged talk radio and cable news programs, it's an understandable impulse to discuss these issues at work, especially around election time. But talking politics on the job is not ethically intelligent.

The Fearsome Foursome

Politics is a pillar of what I call the Fearsome Foursome topics of conversation. The others are sex, money, and religion. All four share certain characteristics:

- Each arouses strong feelings and deeply held beliefs.
- Each is associated with intensely personal values.
- It is difficult to have a rational discussion about each of these topics.

The most sensitive of the Fearsome Foursome is money. You'd probably be more willing to tell a coworker the problems you're having in your sex life than to reveal how much you make a year. As emotionally charged as the topic of sex is, our financial status is an even more volatile one. Most of us feel that we don't have enough money, we worry about being able to pay our bills, and we're filled with anxiety about our retirement accounts (and with good reason, since the Wall Street scandals destroyed many of them).

Religion is another topic that is characterized by more divisiveness than consensus. Even though, as we saw in chapter 1, religious traditions are founded on the same ethical principles,[2] discussions about religion are fraught with dangers, even between two people of the same faith.

But all topics in the Fearsome Foursome are inappropriate for workplace discussion because each one presents ready opportunities for violating the first principle of ethical intelligence, Do No Harm. Discussing any of them can cause harm to your relationships with coworkers, supervisors, and those who report to you; in addition, your own future at the organization can be put in jeopardy.

I'll present two scenarios that illustrate these risks.

Scenario 1: When Coworkers Discuss Politics

Suppose that the race for the White House is under way, and each of the three leading parties has chosen its candidate — Pete Cochran, Linc Hayes, and Julie Barnes. (These happen to be the names of the members of the Mod Squad[3] and do not intentionally refer to any real political candidate or party.) Also, I'll refer to the hot-button topic in question as "XYZ," which can stand for any law or public policy related in some way to violence.

Dave, Ari, Carol, and Miwa work in four conjoined cubicles. Dave is bored, so he strikes up a conversation with Ari.

DAVE. Hey, Ari, did you watch the debate last night?

ARI. Yeah. Linc Hayes won, hands down.

DAVE. Linc Hayes? That guy's a nitwit. He's for XYZ.

ARI. He's right. We'd have a lot less violence everywhere if we had more XYZ. *(Carol tries to focus on her work, but the issue of violence is a sensitive topic for her because a close family member died violently. She does her best to ignore Dave and Ari's discussion.)*

DAVE. Julie Barnes should be our next president. She's against XYZ. Less XYZ is the only way to reduce violence. I checked the studies she talked about, and she's right: XYZ is the problem, not the solution.

ARI. Julie Barnes? First of all, a woman will never be elected president in this country, so a vote for her is a vote thrown away. *(Carol and Ari have worked together on several projects, but she never knew that Ari was for XYZ and viewed women in politics unfavorably.)*

DAVE. Ari, you're being sexist.

ARI, *louder than before.* I am *not* sexist. I'm just realistic about who can win. You've got your head in the sand if you think Julie Barnes stands a chance.

While Dave and Ari's conversation escalates in intensity, Miwa is on the phone with one of her clients. She finds her colleagues' discussion more interesting than the one with her client. She can't wait for the phone call to end so that she can join in, because she has very strong feelings about XYZ.

In the course of a few minutes, Carol has decided she doesn't want to work with Ari, Miwa's attention has drifted away from her client, and Dave and Ari have dropped their work altogether.

This scenario is hardly the stuff of fantasy, and the way it progressed would be the case for any controversial political topic, not just XYZ. Note that both Dave and Ari want the same thing — less violence in society — but disagree strongly about how to achieve this goal. Even when two people want to get from A to B, the way to get there isn't always clear. That's why political discussions — which at their core are often about how to get from A to B — are so fraught with disagreement. It doesn't matter what the political topic happens to be. The result is the same: talking about such matters at work makes it difficult to get one's job done, and it can strain relationships that had previously been good ones.

Scenario 2: When the Boss Talks Politics

At the end of the day, Carol goes to her boss's office to discuss a big project coming up. In the middle of the discussion, the boss casually mentions the political debate from last night.

BOSS. So did you catch the debate?

CAROL, *trying to avoid a repeat of what happened between Dave and Ari.* Um, yeah. I have a question, though, about this proj———.

BOSS. What'd you think of Linc Hayes? He won, hands down.

CAROL, *becoming increasingly uncomfortable.* It was a good debate, I'll say that.

BOSS, *no longer interested in talking about the project.* No, it wasn't! And I'll tell you why. Our country is in trouble. You know that, don't you? *(Carol has never talked politics with her boss before, and she doesn't want to talk about it now, either.)*

CAROL. The thing is, I'm not sure how to deal with this client———.

BOSS. I'll tell you why I like Linc Hayes. Among other things, he's the only one with the courage to support XYZ. That's the only way we're going to reduce violence. You agree with me, right? *(Carol is turning red now. In spite of her best efforts to talk about the project, she feels compelled to take a position.)*

CAROL. Actually, I think Pete Cochran's attitude toward XYZ is the right one.

BOSS. Pete Cochran? Are you serious? That guy is a complete nincompoop. His approach is going to increase violence, not reduce it.

Carol is now angry with her boss, both for dragging her into a political discussion and for supporting a different candidate. When she finally gets back to talking about the project at hand, she finds it hard to keep her mind on it. Her boss finishes the conversation by announcing that he's going to put Ari on the project with Carol because she and Ari have worked well together before.

Carol wonders whether she should tell her boss that she'd rather not work with Ari now. But she suspects she'd be pressed to give her reason, which would just create more tension all around. Carol also wonders if her boss is assigning Ari because Ari is the best person to work on the project or because the two men have similar political convictions.

As election day approaches, Carol's boss continues to chide her for supporting Pete rather than Linc.

Her performance review comes around, and Carol's boss doesn't mention politics. But shortly thereafter, Carol is surprised to discover that her boss has not recommended her for a raise, even though she believes her work has been exceptional and she has the evidence to support her belief.

This scenario is even more troubling than the previous one because much more is at stake. It was bad enough when a political discussion distracted four coworkers, but now, one of those employees may have been denied a raise because of political differences with her boss. There is a striking parallel here with the issue of office romances involving a person who has power over another. Just as an employee who breaks up with her boss and is denied a raise or promotion can never be sure that the bad romance wasn't the culprit, Carol will never know whether her politics was the reason her boss decided against a salary increase.

Isn't There an Upside to Political Discussions on the Job?

Yes, it's possible to have a rational, respectful discussion about political issues, even the hot-button ones, while at work. Hearing a colleague or boss talk about a topic like XYZ can help you understand competing points of view and perhaps become more sympathetic to those who hold positions different from your own. It's even possible for you to change your mind when presented with strong counterarguments to your own position. Perhaps your coworkers have information that you haven't considered, and those facts might make you reconsider where you stand. Even if you don't end up changing your mind, listening nonjudgmentally to those with different points of view is a sign of maturity and good character.

But because political topics and elections stir up such strong emotions, and because it's difficult to be reasonable and respectful when such emotions are aroused, talking politics at work is not consistent with ethical intelligence. Even if a majority of your colleagues are capable of engaging in thoughtful discussions, all it takes is one person getting wound up, and the problems begin.

Why are workplace discussions about politics so problematic compared with topics such as TV, music, movies, and food? For one thing, many people consider aesthetic judgments to be merely a matter of opinion. If you like Madonna and I like The Who, you may not share my taste for hard rock, but you probably don't think I'm wrong for liking it. But if you support the political issue XYZ and I'm against it, you don't think that I hold a different but equally valid point of view; you think I'm mistaken, and as a result, you may think less of me, which could strain our working relationship.[4]

There's also more at stake in politics than in other realms. When the Mars company discontinued production of red M&M's for a decade,[5] fans of the colored treat were disappointed, but their lives weren't ruined. You could have a lively debate with colleagues about the wisdom of this decision, and no one would be the worse for it. However, if another candy company were to cease all operations in the United States and expand its facilities in other countries, tens of thousands of people would lose their jobs, which would have a tremendous negative impact on families across the nation. Some of those affected may be related to your coworkers — or to you. Debating the wisdom of *that* corporate decision presents a much greater challenge to workplace harmony since the stakes are much higher.[6]

Besides, most political discussions have little, if anything, to do with the work at hand. It's simply too easy to get sidetracked, and remain there, when the talk turns to politics. Ethically intelligent managers will discourage, if not prohibit, discussing politics on the job. When a supervisor isn't around and a political topic comes up, the ethically intelligent employee will divert the discussion to less controversial matters. If a few folks are determined to argue about politics and it becomes difficult to do one's job, then the ethically intelligent response is to let a supervisor know what's going on and to ask for an intervention.

Even if there is a legal right to talk about politics (or any of the other Fearsome Foursome topics), it doesn't follow that it's appropriate or wise to do so. And it isn't, because of the risk of harm to relationships with clients, colleagues, and supervisors.

Bottom line: Political discussions at work make it too easy to violate the first principle of ethical intelligence, Do No Harm, as well as the third principle, Respect Others. There is a time and a place for such talk — before coming to the office and after leaving it. As tempting as it may be to debate political issues at work, the ethically intelligent practice is not to do so.

SUFFERING FOOLS GLADLY:
HOW TO DEAL WITH PEOPLE YOU CAN'T STAND

Louise was one of the nastiest people I'd ever met. The overwhelming majority of the things coming out of her mouth were complaints of some sort, and no target was spared. Clients, coworkers, the weather — you name it, she complained about it. It surprised me that Louise had any friends at all since, by all appearances, she never had a good word to say about anybody or anything.

I did my best to stay clear of Louise, but it was impossible to avoid her completely. There was a small kitchen where some of us would have lunch, and inevitably she'd bring her sour spirit to mealtimes. I couldn't understand why no one else seemed to be bothered by her constant barrage of negativity, but people just seemed to take her in stride.

As my work with the company progressed, Louise's backstory began to emerge: She'd come to this country with nothing and had worked as a housekeeper for one of the in-house counsel. Her sponsor sent her to school and found a position for her within the company, where she ended up doing well. I began to see Louise differently; there was a reason why she presented a troubled persona to the world, and it was a good reason. She'd had a tough life.

Before I passed judgment on Louise, I should have remembered what Elvis sang in "Walk a Mile in My Shoes" or what Atticus Finch told his daughter, Scout, in *To Kill a Mockingbird*: "You never really understand a person until you consider things from his point of view...until you climb into his skin and walk around in it."[7] Once I had a better understanding of Louise's story, I became more sympathetic to her, which she may have sensed; one day, I ran into her on the street, and she gave me a big, warm hug. That sealed the deal: I would stop thinking harshly of Louise from that moment on.

The Fifth Principle of Ethical Intelligence:
Easy to Say, Hard to Live By

It's easy to be kind or loving to someone you like. The challenge for living with ethical intelligence is to do so when you have to deal with someone you can't stand. Why should you bother to be loving toward the contemptuous, the hateful, the miserable, or people who are simply annoying?

The answer, in part, is that being loving toward others simply makes you feel better. Isn't that reason enough to adopt a loving attitude in everything you do? It would be narcissistic, though, to say that the only reason to live with ethical intelligence is because it benefits you. This is indeed the case, but there is another good reason: all human beings have an inherent dignity, and your conscious choice to be a loving and kind person is a powerful way to honor that dignity.

As we saw in chapter 2, the first four principles of ethical intelligence — Do No Harm, Make Things Better, Respect Others, and Be Fair — may be properly seen as principles of duty, whereas the fifth principle, Be Loving, is an ideal to which we should aspire. You can be faulted for intentionally harming someone, but it's a stretch to say you're acting unethically if you're not loving to everyone you meet (especially the nasty and the unpleasant).

Nevertheless, ethical intelligence is a critical component of being fully human. To be ethically intelligent is to be committed to bringing out the best in others,[8] which happens to bring out the best in you, too. So even if it is not, strictly speaking, ethically required that we be loving and compassionate to all, the ethically intelligent person recognizes it's important and strives to do so as much as possible.

The challenge presented by the fifth principle of ethical intelligence is ultimately not the intellectual one of justifying it but the practical one of living by it. Even when you know it's a good thing to be loving and kind to all, how can you do so with people who appear to have no interest in reciprocating?

In other words, how can you find a way to be a loving person in those situations where it would be much easier to be mean, spiteful, or antagonistic? Although I recognize how supremely difficult it is, here are my humble suggestions on how to do so.

Being Loving in Everyday Life

1. *Look at the world through the other person's eyes.* In the 1989 film *Dead Poets Society*, new teacher John Keating (played by Robin Williams) has each student stand up on his desk and look at the world from a new perspective. This simple exercise has profound implications when it comes to applying the fifth principle of ethical intelligence. It's not easy to be loving toward the people who push your buttons, but seeing the world the way they do is a huge step in the right direction.

2. *It's usually not about you.* What I learned from my experience with Louise is that what seemed to be hostility directed toward me and everyone else was actually an expression of her own frustrations. This speaks to one of Don Miguel Ruiz's Four Agreements: "Don't take anything personally."[9] (I was offended by this suggestion until I realized he wasn't speaking to me directly.)

3. *Ask for help.* During my workshops, I ask for volunteers to present ethical problems they're facing, because the collective wisdom in the room can provide solutions they wouldn't have thought of on their own. Dispassionate observers aren't emotionally invested in the problem and often come up with creative ways of getting past it.

It also helps when someone says, "This happened to me, and here is how I handled it." It's good to know you're not alone.

4. *Being kinder to yourself makes it easier to be kinder to others.* The converse is also true, as Mark Twain noted: "The best way to cheer yourself up is to try to cheer somebody else up."[10]

5. *Some people are going to be miserable, no matter what you do.* It would be terrific if your best efforts to be kind and compassionate to all prompted others to do the same — but it won't. Rather than get angry at these people, you're better off not making enemies and wasting your energy, following Sir Mick Jagger's advice in the song "Let's Work." I've found that having hateful feelings toward people who have wronged me does nothing to them but a lot of damage to me. Better to set those feelings aside and focus on better, more important things.

SUMMARY

Here's how to be ethically intelligent with your coworkers.

Office Romances

Because they risk violating the Do No Harm principle of ethical intelligence, office romances are not a good idea, however tempting they may be. Employees who cannot resist the call should not work on the same team.

Ethical intelligence is not compatible with office romances characterized by an imbalance of power.

Talking Politics on the Job

Politics, sex, religion, and money constitute the Fearsome Four-some: topics that are ethically unintelligent to discuss at work because of the potential for harming working relationships and diverting attention from the job at hand.

Dealing with People You Can't Stand

It's easy to be compassionate toward people we like. Finding a way to apply the fifth principle of ethical intelligence to those who rub us the wrong way is a formidable challenge — but not an insurmountable one. An ethically intelligent response to working peaceably with off-putting coworkers is to look at the world through their eyes. Appreciating the burdens they carry can help us understand why they are unpleasant to be around and may result in a better relationship with them.

CHAPTER 6

Are You a Good Leader?

Ethical Intelligence
with the People Who Work *for* You

Now that we've considered better and worse ways of dealing with people largely at the same level of power and influence as you, let's look at how you might make the most of your relationships with those who wield less power. We'll examine these issues:

- Giving criticism
- Downsizing and firing staff members
- Handling unpaid internships

GIVING CRITICISM

It was the weekly team meeting, a Friday no different from any other. My friend John; his boss, Cheryl; and John's assistant, Minsun, were planning their work for the following week. John made a casual remark about the prestigious grant he'd recently been awarded, when suddenly Cheryl exploded.

"All I've been hearing about for weeks is your grant!" she blurted, which apparently was quite uncharacteristic of her. John had never seen his boss show any anger, let alone say something like this, and the two had been working together for years.

Cheryl stopped yelling, and John became uncharacteristically quiet. This anger had obviously been simmering for a while, and it erupted violently. John confessed to me that he had indeed been talking a lot about the project for which he'd been given funds. It was valuable to his career, and he had worked really hard to get it. He also admitted that even though the organization had agreed to give him some time off each week to work on the project, he was probably spending too many hours on it. Cheryl was right; John had his priorities in the wrong order.

Nevertheless, Cheryl could have presented her criticism in a more respectful manner. John was embarrassed to be dressed down in front of his assistant. Surely, Minsun didn't have to be in on the bloodletting.

Cheryl did prompt John to rethink his priorities, but her style of criticism wasn't ethically intelligent.

What Is Criticism All About?

There are lots of reasons you may feel compelled to criticize various people on your team:

- They've done something work-related that they shouldn't have done.
- They haven't done something work-related that they should have done.
- They have unpleasant or obnoxious personal habits.
- They get on your nerves.
- You just don't like them.

Accordingly, there are several things you might accomplish through criticism:

- Help the people in question get back on track.
- Make them feel bad for what they did or didn't do.
- Remind them of your power or authority.
- Inspire or motivate them to do better work.

- Let them know that you don't like them.
- Display how clever, smart, witty, or perturbed you are.
- Blow off some steam.

Not all of these goals are consistent with ethical intelligence. Flaunting your power does nothing to improve the situation and is thus a violation of principle 2, Make Things Better. Instilling guilt, fear, or other negative feelings simply because you can, or because it makes you feel better, is a violation of principle 1, Do No Harm. (This isn't to say that it's always wrong if someone feels bad after being criticized. In fact, feeling guilt or shame in the appropriate degree is a good sign — namely, that one has a conscience, a sense of pride, or a commitment to being responsible.)

Shouting in anger, launching into creative invectives, or cutting someone down to size doesn't honor any of the five principles of ethical intelligence. In fact, the Buddhist monk and author Thich Nhat Hanh argues persuasively that venting actually makes one feel worse.[1] Criticizing someone merely to feel better about yourself doesn't accomplish that objective. Nobody wins.

The only kind of criticism that is consistent with ethical intelligence is criticism that seeks to bring out the best in people. It is the quintessential way to apply principle 2 at work (or anywhere else, for that matter). When one has power over someone else, the ethically intelligent thing to do is to use that power imbalance constructively and seek to make things better, not worse. In the scenario at the beginning of this section, Cheryl's outburst was more about her own frustration than about helping John get back on track. It's understandable to be frustrated when a subordinate isn't doing his or her best work, but ethically intelligent criticism is given, first and foremost, with an eye toward improving the other person, for that person's sake and the sake of others, too.

How to Give Ethically Intelligent Criticism

Here is how to give criticism that brings out the best in others —
and yourself.

1. *Find the right setting.* Cheryl was right to criticize John, but she
shouldn't have done so in front of John's assistant.

2. *Start with something positive.* Surely there is something praiseworthy that the person has done recently, and it's a good idea to
start the criticism with it. Cheryl might have begun by saying that
she was glad John had gotten the grant he had worked so long and
hard to earn. Starting with praise is good from both an ethical and
a psychological point of view. Ethically, it upholds principle 4, Be
Fair, since it gives others their due. Psychologically, it makes them
receptive to what you're about to say.

3. *Focus on the behavior, not the person.* The most effective way to
elevate, to inspire, and to promote excellence is to narrow your field
of vision to the problem before you. A good visual metaphor is a
shrinking circle, like the kind you see in old movies to transition
from the end of one scene to the beginning of the next one (which,
in moving from praise to criticism, you are in fact doing). If you're
troubled by a team member's work ethic — coming to work late,
leaving early, goofing off on the job — calling him or her lazy, self-
ish, or a goofball is more hurtful than helpful. It's also probably
untrue; presumably there were good reasons to hire this person, he
or she has done good work in the past, and outside of work, you're
likely to find the person full of energy and commitment.

For example, instead of saying, "You're a goof-off," you could
say, "You've been coming to work late too often, and when you're
here, you spend too much time on personal matters." The first is an
insult; the second is a valid complaint about specific, inappropriate
behavior.

4. *End on an inspiring note.* If this is a first offense and it's not especially egregious, there is no point in giving an ultimatum, which is
really nothing more than a threat. Instead of an explicit or implicit
"You'd better get your act together, or else," it is better to give your
vote of confidence. People rise — or sink — to the level expected
of them. The ethically intelligent critic seeks not to frighten but to
inspire.

If you find yourself in Cheryl's position someday, the ethically
intelligent response would be to speak privately to the troublesome
employee, praise that person's contributions, mention specific concerns you have, and affirm your belief in him or her. More than
likely, the employee will make changes for the better.

One thing life has taught me is that people will pleasantly surprise you if you only give them the chance.

DOWNSIZING WITH DIGNITY, FIRING WITH FINESSE

A friend of mine who works at a large bank told me that some of
his coworkers found out that they'd been downsized when they
couldn't log on to their computers in the morning. Is this an ethically intelligent way to let someone go?

Of course not. In fact, it's hard to imagine a less compassionate way of giving someone bad news. Terminations by phone and
email are not uncommon, and surely by now at least one person has
been let go by a text message.

Managers who use these techniques claim that it's easier than
having a messy, unpleasant person-to-person conversation. It is
easier — but for whom? Certainly not the employee on the receiving end. Recall the discussion in chapter 2 about better and worse
ways to apply the Minimize Unavoidable Harm corollary to Do No
Harm in the dating arena: there are better and worse ways to let

someone know you're not interested in going out with him or her again. The ethically intelligent person who decides not to pursue a romantic relationship with someone takes the Minimize Unavoidable Harm rule to heart and acts accordingly. The same is true for ethically intelligent managers who must end someone's term of employment.

Downsizing versus Firing

People who have been downsized have told me that they bristle at the term *fired* and don't believe it's applicable to their situation. They have a point. To be downsized is to be let go from an organization for reasons other than one's performance. Usually, the justification is the state of the economy, but there are other possible reasons as well, such as changes in the nature of the business itself. Thousands of employees at the Eastman Kodak Company in Rochester, New York, were let go when the digital revolution made traditional photography less popular and much of the work associated with the older model was no longer necessary.[2] The Kodak employees lost their jobs through no fault of their own, so the term *downsizing* seems fitting for this unfortunate turn of events.

Firing, on the other hand, implies fault, and there is a continuum of blame to consider. On one end of the spectrum lies poor or inadequate performance. At the other extreme is criminal and flagrantly unethical behavior: fraud, theft, sexual or racial harassment, and the like. There is an ethically relevant difference between an employee being let go because the company has phased out his job and the company letting him go because it discovered that he used corporate funds for whiskey-soaked junkets to Vegas.

Let's now consider how managers can use the principles of ethical intelligence effectively when they are called upon to downsize or fire an employee.

Five Rules for Downsizing with Dignity and Firing with Finesse

The following techniques for downsizing and firing both minimize unavoidable harm and, as with ethically intelligent criticism, bring out the best in the people who use them.

1. *Do it in person whenever possible.* As uncomfortable as it is to end someone's employment, the right thing to do is to have a private conversation with him or her in person. An in-person conversation upholds the third principle of ethical intelligence, Respect Others; emails, phone calls, and other mediated forms of communication do not. Also, the fifth principle of ethical intelligence, Be Loving, calls upon you to treat others with kindness and compassion, and a face-to-face meeting is the best way to apply that principle when you must let an employee go.

Of course, there are situations in which it is impractical to do this. The head of sales for a company I know had to lay off three people who lived in different parts of the country, and it simply wasn't possible for her to meet with each employee. In this sort of case, a conversation by phone or Internet video is, by default, acceptable. It's better than downsizing by email or text, because the Minimize Unavoidable Harm rule still applies.

2. *Do it privately.* To show respect for a person — that is, to apply the third principle of ethical intelligence — is to honor that person's values and preferences. It's reasonable to assume that most people would prefer to have troubling news delivered in private. This means that if you're the one giving the bad news, you do so in your office, with the door closed. I've heard of managers who made their move at the employee's cubicle within earshot of everyone in the vicinity. Isn't this simply a matter of common sense and decency?

3. *Give the person your full attention.* Interrupting the conversation to take phone calls, check your BlackBerry, or engage in other

distractions tells the other person that the matter at hand isn't all that important to you. That's yet another violation of the principle of respect. The impulse to turn your attention to less troubling matters is understandable; but along with the privileges of being a manager come responsibilities, and one such responsibility is having integrity when you must let an employee go.

4. *Be honest, but not brutally so.* Must you always tell the truth, the whole truth, and nothing but the truth? We considered this important question in chapter 2. Yes, if you're giving sworn testimony in a legal deposition or court of law, you must be completely truthful, but beyond these situations, the duty to tell the truth is constrained by the duty to minimize harm. In practical terms, this means being forthright with the employee but also choosing with care the words, tone of voice, and demeanor you use. *Compassion* is an aspect of the fifth principle of ethical intelligence, Be Loving, and it literally means "suffering with" someone. Showing compassion both honors the dignity of other people and speaks to the better part of your nature. Finally, consider the first principle of ethical intelligence, Do No Harm. We can't always make things better, but we shouldn't make things worse.

For example, if you have to let Joe go because his sales performance was in the bottom 10 percent, you should mention this, but there's no reason to add that his jokes are lame, his laugh is annoying, or his hairpiece is horrendous.

5. *Don't rush.* A shock takes time to absorb. Imagine that your physician says you have a serious illness. Wouldn't you expect him or her to allow the news to sink in rather than to summarily dismiss you and call for the next patient? Being let go isn't as serious as getting a diagnosis of cancer or heart disease, but it is still a major, life-changing event. You owe your employee the time to absorb the information, and you may have to explain more than once what is

happening and why. You would demand nothing less if it were happening to you, and you would be right to do so.

You versus Your Organization

The five rules presented in the previous section assume that your organization has good reasons for downsizing. But what if you don't see things this way? Suppose, for example, that your company believes it's necessary to shift its customer service jobs overseas, and you believe that doing so is both unethical and bad for business. In this case, you not only have a right to object; you have an ethical obligation to do so.

Does this mean that you should be prepared to give up your job to make your point? Not necessarily. Depending on your personal circumstances, your duties to your family or to yourself might justifiably override the value of making a statement by quitting. Even if you are committed to keeping as many jobs as possible in your community, this goal will take time to achieve, and it may be easier to do so from within the company than from the outside. One person *can* make a difference, but when the obstacles are formidable, as they are here, you might be more likely to bring about the change you seek by remaining an employee of the organization. Doing so also allows you to honor your financial responsibilities to your family or yourself.

Revenue is important, but so are the values of respect, compassion, and simple decency. The ethically intelligent manager takes all of these into account — always.

THE HANNIBAL LECTER SYNDROME: THE ETHICS OF UNPAID INTERNSHIPS

In a key scene from the film *The Silence of the Lambs*, FBI agent Clarice Starling interviews the serial killer Hannibal Lecter in prison and asks him for help in solving a case that concerns a crime similar to what Lecter committed.

"Quid pro quo," Lecter tells Starling. He'll help her on the condition that she reveal something intensely personal about herself.

The Latin phrase that Lecter uses means "something for something." It applies not just to the kind of relationship he wants with his interrogator but to any sort of arrangement between two people in which each wants or needs something from the other. One such arrangement is that staple of summer work across the country, the unpaid internship. Is it wrong not to pay the interns who work for you? Let's take a look.

Are Quid Pro Quo Relationships Necessarily Unethical?

In chapter 5, I argued that office romances were generally inconsistent with ethical intelligence because of the dangers these relationships present to colleagues, clients, the organization, and the lovers themselves. Of special concern is the office romance between a boss and his or her subordinate since this type of romance raises the possibility of sexual harassment. One type of sexual harassment recognized by the law occurs when a boss offers a subordinate employment benefits in exchange for sex. This is a quid pro quo arrangement at its most blatantly unethical since it is both exploitative and illegal.

But some quid pro quo relationships are ethically intelligent. Consider this exchange between you and your spouse:

You. Let's go to the football game on Sunday.

Spouse. You know I don't care much for football.

You. Tell you what: if you'll go to the game with me, I'll see that movie you've been wanting to see. Deal?

Spouse. Deal!

This quid pro quo agreement is in accordance with the principles of ethical intelligence. Each person is free to accept or reject the offer that the other one makes. There is a balance of power between the two parties, and neither one is taking advantage of the other. The arrangement is both respectful (because neither party is being treated merely as a means to an end) and fair (because each person is getting his or her due).

Unpaid internships are a form of quid pro quo arrangements. A business or other organization offers experience to someone and in turn receives help from that person. It's the *kind* of experience the person gains that determines whether a particular unpaid internship is ethical or not. If what the intern does is integral to learning about the enterprise (for example, setting up appointments and then attending those meetings), this is valuable to the intern and is thus ethically appropriate. If, however, the intern is acting essentially as unpaid labor (for example, by stuffing envelopes, making photocopies, or fetching coffee), such work may constitute exploitation and is therefore to be avoided.

Note that it isn't the lack of payment or the imbalance of power per se that makes some unpaid internships ethically questionable or flat-out wrong. When an organization offers a useful experience to a young person that he or she might not be able to get any other way, the knowledge or skills that are gained may legitimately take the place of a paycheck, college credit, or other tangible benefit.

I speak from experience. During the spring break of my junior year in college, I spent the entire week as an intern for a physician at the University of Pennsylvania. Although I had little contact with the doctor, I had my first taste of doing professional research, and I loved it. I didn't mind that I wasn't being paid, or even that my week was spent in a library rather than at the beach. The passion I discovered I had for doing such work continues to this day. If I had simply been answering phones, without any exposure to the substance of the physician's work, I wouldn't have learned anything relevant to the practice of medicine, and the arrangement would have been unfair.

Five Rules for Creating and Managing Unpaid Internships with Ethical Intelligence

If you're considering bringing interns aboard and not paying them, here are some guidelines for doing so with ethical intelligence.

1. *Make sure the intern is going to gain something genuinely useful.* Going on sales calls, learning how to use public relations tools, and being part of discussions with you and other managers about your business are just some of the things that can be meaningful to someone who is considering going into your line of work.

2. *Don't have interns do menial labor if you're not going to pay them for it.* Having your interns do nothing but refill the coffee pot or run errands takes advantage of your power over them and may even be illegal. According to B. David Joffe, an employment law expert at the law firm Bradley Arant Boult Cummings, "Under the Fair Labor Standards Act, the U.S. Labor Department generally takes the position that it is not permissible for an individual to volunteer his or her services to a for-profit employer."[3] Joffe also notes that in certain circumstances, students obtaining training are not considered to be employees and thus are not covered under the Fair Labor Standards Act. Payment generally isn't necessary for students and others who are being trained, but menial labor provided to a for-profit employer does ordinarily require financial compensation.[4]

3. *Express your gratitude — often.* It's always the right time to say thanks. Even if you can't pay your interns, you can still do something nice for them, such as take them out to lunch from time to time, give them gift cards, or something else along these lines. Of course, such gestures apply to everyone on your team. And the best form of gratitude, for most people, is still a paycheck.

4. *Resist taking on a friend's son or daughter.* As we saw with one of the quiz questions in chapter 1, dual relationships are sticky, and

you may find your friendship compromised if the internship doesn't work out. Nepotism is common, but that doesn't mean it's good for business or good for you. Just because a practice is accepted doesn't mean it is acceptable.

5. *Make it clear to the intern early on what he or she can expect to accomplish through the experience and what won't be on the agenda.* The saying "An ounce of prevention is worth a pound of cure" is a cliché because it's true. There aren't likely to be misunderstandings between you and your interns later if you explain up front what the internship is going to entail.

Bottom line: Unpaid internships have gotten a bad rap and, in many cases, for good reason. But by the example you set, you can show the business world not only that it is possible to do these the right way but that everyone wins when such arrangements are founded on the ethical principles of respect and fairness, two pillars of ethical intelligence. The imbalance of power between you and your intern need not result in exploitation, and if you follow the guidelines above, it won't.

SUMMARY

Here's how to be ethically intelligent with the people who work for you.

Giving Criticism

Ethically intelligent criticism helps the person being criticized and does not flaunt the power of the critic. It focuses on specific things the person in question can do better and includes recognition of what that person does well.

Downsizing with Dignity, Firing with Finesse

When you're called upon to let employees go, whether or not their performance is the cause of their being terminated, the ethically intelligent way to do so is in person, whenever possible. Giving employees the time to absorb the shock is both compassionate and essential.

When you believe the termination isn't justified, the principle of fairness requires you to speak up and consider other ways of helping the organization move forward.

Unpaid Internships

It is ethically intelligent to bring interns aboard and not pay them, as long as the interns get something of value from the experience and are not there merely to provide free labor.

CHAPTER 7

You're Not the Boss of Me!
Oh, Wait a Second — You Are
Ethical Intelligence with Your Boss

S uccess at work means dealing effectively not just with those who have less power than you but also with those who have power over you. We'll now consider how to be ethically intelligent when your boss:

- Says offensive things at work
- Criticizes you
- Gives you an assignment you object to
- Reveals that he or she has a problem with drugs or alcohol

THE TRASH-TALKING BOSS

A friend of mine — I'll call her Barbara — works in the executive offices of a popular chain of grocery stores. Her boss — let's call him Al — loves to tell jokes, and he tells them frequently. The problem with Al's jokes is that they offend entire groups of people: women, gays, lesbians, African Americans, Jews, the disabled — Al makes fun of them all. Al's defense is that he is an equal opportunity offender, so he's not singling out any particular group. Barbara has been known to tell an off-color joke or two herself, but she takes care not to do so while on the job.

Last week, Al told Barbara that because of changes in company policy, both of them would be getting lower performance reviews this year, although each would be getting a raise. When Barbara expressed dismay at the lower rating, Al assured her that the important thing is that she would be getting more money.

"Barbara, you're a whore, just like me!" he said with a smirk.

Barbara usually ignores Al's locker-room style of humor, but this time she had to speak up.

"Wait a second, Al. Let me write that down for the lawsuit I plan to file."

The normally talkative Al was caught off guard and stopped speaking for a moment. "Er," he sputtered, "you know I'm only kidding."

After an awkward silence, they moved on to discuss an assignment Al had given Barbara to do.

Al's comment is a straightforward example of how to violate the first principle of ethical intelligence, Do No Harm, while at work. Although Al's salty language constitutes an offense, not a harm per se, his churlish sense of humor may indeed interfere with Barbara's ability to work well with him and to do her job to the best of her abilities. It isn't a stretch, then, to suggest that Al's boorish behavior harms his relationship with his direct report (and who knows how many others within his purview). Both the company for which they work and the customers they serve may ultimately be worse off because of Al's trash talk.

Al's claim that he meant no harm doesn't let him off the hook. As the familiar expression says, "The road to hell is paved with good intentions."

The Boss as Leader

Whether Al likes it or not, his behavior sets the standards for how the people he manages comport themselves. If Al is known to tell racist, sexist, or homophobic jokes while on the job, he is essentially telling the office, "I'm not troubled by them, so feel free to indulge in them, too." Being a manager brings with it some great benefits: a higher salary, the prestige associated with holding an influential position, and sometimes even a dedicated parking space. But with these benefits come responsibilities, and all of these duties are related in some way to ethical intelligence.

The ethically intelligent boss is, above all else, a leader committed to the principles Do No Harm, Make Things Better, Respect Others, Be Fair, and Be Loving. Having an ethically intelligent boss doesn't guarantee that all team members will be committed to those principles, but an ethically unintelligent one all but guarantees that everyone else will not be at their best. At the very least, the disturbing lack of self-awareness that a boss like Al exhibits presents an obstacle to getting one's work done well.

Jokes: The Good, the Bad, and the Ugly

Ethical intelligence does not call for a workplace devoid of jokes and laughter. An office without an ounce of merriment would be a dreary place to be, and such an atmosphere could itself be a detriment to working effectively. What kinds of jokes are acceptable, and what should be considered off limits?

In chapter 5, I suggested that talking about the Fearsome Foursome — sex, money, politics, and religion — is not consistent with ethical intelligence because of the potential for harm to occur. It makes sense, then, that jokes about Fearsome Foursome topics should similarly be put on hold until after work (if they're to be told at all). But there are other subjects that don't make for ethically intelligent jokes in the workplace. Federal laws such as Title VII of the Civil Rights Act of 1964, the Age Discrimination in Employment Act of 1967, and the Americans with Disabilities Act of 1990 prohibit discrimination based on race, color, religion, sex, national origin, age, and disability. But even if your organization is not covered by these laws, joking in the workplace about members of such groups is not ethically intelligent. Such jokes risk violating the Do No Harm and Respect Others principles, and they're not kind or compassionate, either.

If your boss has a habit of making jokes that are rude, offensive, or mean-spirited, you have a right to encourage him or her to stop. Recall from chapter 2 that the first principle of ethical intelligence, Do No Harm, has an important corollary: Prevent Harm. One of the reasons that Al, the grocery store executive, trash-talks so often is probably because no one has called him on it (or no one did until Barbara stepped up to the plate). But old habits die hard, and if your boss simply won't put an end to this boorish behavior, it may be necessary to get human resources or the designated office or person in the organization involved. It's reasonable to have human resources take over, in part because this sort of problem is within their purview and also because it's sensible to maintain a good working relationship with a boss, even a coarse one. As I'll discuss in the next section, everyone should welcome constructive criticism (even if it comes from a direct report), but your boss might not see things this way and could hold it against you.

The purpose of such an intervention is not to punish Al but to help him become a better manager and set the highest possible standards for conduct while on the job. What Al jokes about at home is his business. What he does at work is everyone's business.

"GET OFF MY BACK!":
WHEN YOUR BOSS CRITICIZES YOU

The first job I had after graduate school was as an assistant professor at a large state university, and on occasion, I was called upon to write book reviews for scholarly publications. It was exciting to be in a position that commanded respect — my words were now going to be read by a worldwide audience, not just by my professors. But part of the thrill had to do with evaluating some of the same people whose work I had read as a student. Not only was I their colleague, but I also had a degree of power over them, which I thought was cool.

My first review was of a book written by someone my boss himself had studied under, and I had both positive and negative things to say about the work. I showed my boss a draft of the review and figured he'd be pleased with what I thought was a thorough, well-written critique.

His response took me by surprise. "Don't take potshots if you don't have to," he said as he pointed out a troublesome passage. I don't remember exactly what I wrote in that portion of the review, but I do know it was more a display of how clever I could be than an on-point discussion about the argument the book's author was making.

Two things about the experience have stayed with me:

1. I learned to be on guard for using my power and authority to cut someone down to size.
2. My boss offered useful criticism without being unpleasant. In fact, it was his restraint that made the criticism so helpful. He modeled the right way to criticize and, in so doing, criticized me with ethical intelligence.

In chapter 6, we looked at ethically intelligent ways of giving criticism to team members. It's now time to turn the tables and reflect upon how to accept valid criticism with ethical intelligence and how to respond when the criticism is wrongheaded, mean-spirited, or downright hostile.

Why It's Hard to Be Criticized

Criticism done well seeks to get someone back on track, to inspire or motivate that person, and to bring out the best in him or her. Why, then, is it so unpleasant to be on the receiving end of *any* criticism, even that of the ethically intelligent variety?

It is extraordinarily difficult to see oneself accurately. No matter what your level of self-esteem is, you probably have a distorted view of who you really are. If your self-regard is in the mid- to high range, you're more likely to notice the things you do well and overlook the things you don't. If your self-esteem is, as Woody Allen, playing Isaac Davis, said to Diane Keaton's character, Mary Wilkie, in *Manhattan*, "a notch below Kafka's," you tend to focus on the mistakes you make and forget or deny the things at which you excel.

Criticism of those with positive self-esteem challenges their view of themselves as beyond reproach, even when the criticism is ethically intelligent. "I can't possibly be so flawed," such a person thinks upon hearing such criticism, and his or her defenses go up. Accurate criticism for the Kafkaesque man or woman merely confirms his or her biggest fear: "I am indeed a flawed person." This hurts, and it's only natural to resist things that cause painful feelings. People with low self-esteem may cover up the sting of criticism by responding with resentment or anger. Any way you slice it, criticism doesn't feel good and is understandably met with resistance.

But it's one thing to appreciate why criticism is unpleasant and another to justify the natural tendency to push it away. When criticism is viewed objectively, apart from the trappings of one's ego, one can see that it's irrational to ignore good criticism. You can always do your job better, no matter how well you actually do it (or think you do). Accepting, even welcoming, ethically intelligent criticism is one of the best ways to grow professionally and personally. Living rationally means, in part, acting prudently, and taking good criticism to heart is simply a prudent thing to do.[1]

What Is Ethically *Un*intelligent Criticism?

As the story about my boss illustrates, it is indeed possible for one's superior to offer criticism with ethical intelligence. But other varieties of criticism seem far more common, and it's worth expanding the scope of our investigation so that we can consider these types of critique. We live in an age where it's possible to leave scathing criticism anonymously on the Internet, where "reality" TV and talk radio programs offer a constant display of the most childish ways to find fault with others, and where political candidates use personal attacks rather than reasoned argument to win elections. It makes sense that the term for personal attacks online is "flaming" someone; the point of such criticism is to hurt, to demean, and to leave scars. And it does.

As a public figure, I receive plenty of personal criticism, and I have to tell you that even though I've been doing my job for many years, such criticism hurts. After I've been interviewed on CNN or written an article for Bloomberg Businessweek online, a few disgruntled people will email me or submit a post filled with invectives, which I won't bother reproducing here. I've noticed several recurring elements of critics who submit these hateful communications:

1. They usually hide behind nicknames and don't provide their true identities.
2. They focus on my personal characteristics, my qualifications as an ethicist, how they themselves feel about me — everything but the arguments I'm making.
3. The nastier and more mean-spirited the criticism is, the more likely it is to be expressed poorly through sloppy

grammar, frequent misspellings, and a tendency to over-use capital letters and exclamation marks.

Why are such critiques ethically unintelligent? First of all, they say nothing about the truth content of the position they're attacking. Ad hominem arguments (arguments in which the object of criticism is the person rather than what he or she is saying) are fallacious. They're not really arguments at all but expressions of raw, unexamined emotions. It doesn't even matter how smart or successful the critic may be; even if William Shakespeare were to respond to my argument against office romances by proclaiming, "Bruce Weinstein is a pribbling, base-court apple-john," it wouldn't follow that anything I've said about the ethics of dating coworkers is wrong. I may indeed be mistaken, but Mr. Shakespeare's attack against my person would say nothing about the validity of the argument I've made, even though his Elizabethan-era insults would make for a poetic zinger.[2]

Another reason why the forms of criticism I've mentioned are ethically unintelligent is that they're intentional violations of the Do No Harm principle. Even though I realize personal criticism has no philosophical validity, being on the receiving end of it still is an unpleasant experience (though I wouldn't mind the occasional Shakespearean slam, if only to enjoy the artistry that went into making it). I know that the kind of people who choose to write vindictive emails that seek not to enlighten but to destroy and who don't even have the courage to be accountable have probably been beaten up in some way themselves — but it still hurts. If those bent on hurting people through Internet communication could see the effects of their actions, or if their identities were revealed in their emails and posts, I suspect that many of them would think twice before hitting Send.[3]

How to Respond to Criticism with Ethical Intelligence

When someone criticizes you, even if it's not your boss, an ethically intelligent response includes doing the following things.

1. *Resist the urge to dismiss the critic.* Considering what the person has to say will only strengthen your own understanding of the issue you care about. It's hard to face your flaws, but if the criticism is offered with ethical intelligence, it's in your own interest to pay attention. If you're receiving the criticism in person, resist the urge to interrupt the critic and defend yourself.

2. *Recognize that you may not be right.* You may be unaware of one or more of the facts relevant to your argument, or you may have ignored some of the rules or principles at stake.

3. *Realize that ad hominem attacks say more about the person making them than about you.* Rather than sink to the level of such attacks, it's wiser to ignore them.

4. *Transform a glass of poison into a healing elixir.* In my lectures, media interviews, and books, I use the personal attacks I've received as examples of how not to give effective criticism. Doing so alleviates their sting and may help others to resist taking the low road themselves. Tina Fey went so far as to put one nasty email on the back cover of her memoir, *Bossypants*,[4] and her humorous discussion of it was prominently featured in the *New York Times* review of the work.[5]

But you don't have to be a public speaker, TV pundit, or celebrity to turn malicious criticism into the stuff of ethical intelligence. Simply being aware of how lousy it feels to receive nasty correspondence can prompt you to avoid being a perpetrator of it. I often struggle with such ignoble impulses myself, so I know how hard it is to put this idea into practice.

5. *Be grateful.* After you've received constructive criticism, the best thing to say is, "Thank you." You've just been given an opportunity to grow, and it's a gift. If you've received ethically unintelligent criticism and you've taken the high road in response to it, you should be grateful for having resisted the impulse to lower yourself to the critic's level.

Our goal in life can be to bring out the best in others and ourselves, or it can be to puff up our own egos and debase others by exploiting our power over them. If the first is our mission, we would do well to give criticism respectfully and receive it graciously whenever it is offered in good faith.

THE TROUBLING ASSIGNMENT

A few years ago, after working in the public relations field for a long time, Matt decided to launch his own firm. It has been a struggle, in part because the firm is based in one of the most competitive markets in the country. Kelsey is the newest member of the staff. Thanks to her superior networking skills, which is one of the main reasons Matt chose her for the position over dozens of other qualified candidates, she has amassed a lot of media connections.

Matt has just brought in a client named Justin, who has a self-published novel called *January: The Cat Who Ate Little Rock*. Having made a fortune in the oil and gas industries, Justin now wants to realize a lifelong dream: to have a bestselling book to his credit. He tells Matt he wants to get on the biggest TV shows, do readings in the country's largest bookstores, and be reviewed in leading newspapers and magazines. When Matt appoints Kelsey as the head of Justin's campaign, Kelsey takes the book home, reads it, and goes to Matt's office first thing in the morning with a major concern.

KELSEY. Matt, this book is horrible! It's easily the worst one I've ever had to represent. Every page is filled with misspellings and sloppy grammar, and — worst of all — the story is ridiculous! An alien cat named January lands in Arkansas and kills everything in its path? Who is going to read this junk? We're leading Justin on if we allow him to believe this book can ever become a bestseller.

MATT. Kelsey, our job isn't to pass judgments on our clients' work. It's to get them as much exposure as possible.

KELSEY. Well, I'm one of the best publicists around, but I'm not a miracle worker! Justin wants to be on the top morning TV programs? He'll be lucky if he can get booked on public access at 2 AM! I'm telling you, there isn't a single reputable outlet that would ever interview this guy.

MATT. Just give it your best shot. We owe him that, at least.

KELSEY. How can I pitch him with a straight face? Besides, I've developed good relationships with my media contacts, and they trust me when I pitch to them. They know I won't waste their time. I have a good reputation, and I want to protect it.

MATT. Kelsey, this job isn't about you — it's about our clients! There are lots of things you can do for Justin. Sign up on Amazon.com for ten different accounts, then leave rave reviews about the book using each account. There are some paid services that will write positive reviews, too. Get on Facebook, Twitter, blogs. We just have to show Justin that his book is getting some publicity. (Pauses.) I know a lot of hungry publicists who wouldn't have a problem with this. Do I have to say more?

Kelsey smiles wanly, leaves Matt's office, and heads out for a coffee, furious about what she has been asked to do. She tries to consider her options but can't focus for long on any of them because she's so angry with her boss.

It's All in a Day's Work, Right?

Kelsey is right to be troubled by what Matt is asking her to do. In the short run, Matt can indeed make some money with people like Justin, but if he makes a habit of it, his company will get a reputation for misrepresenting its clients. Misrepresenting the truth, which violates the third principle of ethical intelligence, not only shows disrespect for other people; it's also disrespectful of one's own enterprise. It's both unethical and bad for business.

Matt's call to plant positive reviews also does a disservice to the people who buy books, without whose support Matt's business would not be possible. Many book lovers use reviews to help them decide which books to buy, and they trust that positive reviews are written by people who actually read and liked the books they're raving about. If a reader can't rely on a review being honest and accurate, rather than paid-for puffery, he or she would have no reason to bother reading reviews at all.

If Matt's public relations plan became an acceptable industry practice, everyone would eventually be the worse for it: readers would have one less source to help them make informed decisions about what to read; authors would have fewer opportunities to get the word out about their work; clients like Justin would rightly feel ripped off for having had their (unrealistic) hopes encouraged and then dashed; and publicists would find it hard to get anyone to believe what they say, which would damage their own reputations and those of the businesses for which they work. In addition to compromising the third principle of ethical intelligence, Matt's campaign violates the first principle, Do No Harm.

When I was a teenager, I was a member of the amateur (or "ham") radio community, in which building one's own gear was a mark of real accomplishment. I'll never forget a passage in one manual I read that tried to steer the less than competent (like me) away from hack work: "There always have been, and there always will be, haywire artists, whose mission is to get the job done, no matter what." Just substitute "unethical bosses" for "haywire artists," and you have an apt description of people like Matt. Although the story I've presented (which is based on a true incident) is set in the world of publicity, unethical assignments can be found in any organization, business, or group — in other words, wherever there are people.

You have doubtless been asked to do something unethical at some time in your career. Perhaps you're wrestling with this problem right now. It's fitting, then, to consider the ethically intelligent way to deal with unethical job assignments.

When Your Boss Gives You an Unethical Assignment

Having a positive relationship with your boss is good for its own sake as well as for the sake of other things, such as raises, promotions, and recommendations to future employers. But you can't rightfully be expected to fulfill ethically objectionable assignments. An ethically intelligent response is one in which you stand up for what's right without jeopardizing the valuable relationship you have with your supervisor. Here's how Kelsey (or you) can accomplish both of these important goals.

1. *Explain to your boss why you believe the assignment is wrong.* It's possible that Matt doesn't know that his campaign ideas for Justin are ethically unintelligent. He may think that because he and some of his colleagues write fake reviews from time to time, it's okay to do this. He may believe that because a practice is accepted, it is acceptable.

Kelsey is right to be angry about this assignment, but her anger has gotten the best of her. It's not easy to think straight when one's emotions are overwhelming. Kelsey is more likely to prevail — and help Matt, his company, and Justin — if she can calmly explain to Matt why his plan is both wrong and bad for business.

She might begin, for example, by agreeing with Matt that she wants to help people like Justin. Matt should understand that Kelsey is on his side. The next step is to show why Matt's plan will hurt, not help, Justin, as well as Matt and his company. Publicists who misrepresent their clients will not only *not* get their clients placed; they will also make it harder for future clients (who may actually have talent) to get booked. Like the boy who cried wolf, it's hard to be believed after making intentionally false claims a number of times, and such a practice can have a greatly undesirable outcome.

Kelsey would do well to end the conversation by presenting some win-win solutions. She could help Justin get a good editor so that his book could be reworked into something that would be more marketable. She could recommend some classes Justin could take or books he could read that would help him sharpen his writing abilities. If Justin balks at such a proposal, Kelsey cannot in good conscience represent him and should refund his money.

2. *Find a way to accomplish the objective of the assignment without compromising your integrity.* Both Kelsey and Matt want to help Justin, and it's possible to do this in an ethically intelligent manner. For example, Kelsey could target the public relations campaign to the niche audience of science fiction and fantasy fans who are also cat lovers, such as readers of blogs devoted to writers like Andre Norton (once Justin's manuscript has been copyedited). It would also be important for Kelsey to manage Justin's expectations. She should tell him that it's possible that some mainstream magazines like *Cat Fancy* and *The Magazine of Fantasy & Science Fiction* would want to apprise their readers of *January: The Cat Who Ate Little Rock* but that appearances on the top national morning TV shows are simply not a realistic goal.

3. *Refuse to do the assignment.* If Matt is a reasonable person — and it's in his own interest to be — he will rethink his campaign ideas. But it's possible that, for whatever reason (greed, hubris, or difficulty accepting criticism from subordinates, women, or both), he'll reject Kelsey's ideas. If he won't take no for an answer, Kelsey must refuse to go along with the plan. Justin's well-being and Kelsey's own reputation are at stake, and she shouldn't violate the first principle of ethical intelligence, Do No Harm, simply to collect a paycheck.

4. *Pick your battles.* Kelsey should take a hard line only if she is convinced this issue is worth fighting for, because by refusing to budge, she could lose her job. It's a sign of her integrity that she is willing to take a stand against an unethical assignment, but only for truly egregious tasks should she seriously consider walking away or being let go. Kelsey could refuse to write bogus reviews but still do other kinds of work on the project.

5. *Keep in mind you may be wrong.* Kelsey would do well to get a reality check from someone she trusts. Perhaps Justin's book isn't as awful as Kelsey thinks it is. It's important to pay attention when one feels the stirrings of injustice; it's also important to ensure that what one believes is wrong really *is* wrong.

THE BOSS WITH A DRINKING PROBLEM

Tom is senior vice president of operations at a large insurance company. At the annual holiday party yesterday for Tom's division, he got drunk and made a fool of himself — again. This is the fourth time in the past six months that Fred, Tom's direct report, has observed such behavior. Tom did the same thing at the past two office parties and once at a bar after work.

Fred has smelled alcohol on Tom's breath during the workday many times but has been reluctant to say anything for fear of

angering Tom and jeopardizing Tom's future at the company —
and Fred's as well. But the holiday party represented a new low:
the more Tom drank, the more inappropriate his behavior became
toward June, the youngest member of the staff. Risqué jokes gave
way to Tom's putting his arm around June and eventually pull-
ing her toward him as if they were romantically involved with one
another. Fred intervened several times, but Tom's behavior continued on its downward spiral.

Last night, Fred couldn't sleep. "How can I be the only one
bothered by this?" he kept asking himself. Several times, he has
heard people at the office talking about it, but they don't seem to
take it very seriously. He also thought about the other senior managers at the company. "Surely," Fred reasoned, "Marla, Rashid, and
Rick know about what's going on with Tom. They're the ones who
should be doing something about this, not me."

Today, Tom shows up late at work and doesn't say anything
about how he had conducted himself. Fred doesn't know what to
do now. He's a few weeks away from getting his yearly bonus, and
Tom has been talking recently about giving Fred a raise. But Fred
is deeply troubled by what is going on with his boss and worries
about the terrible things that could happen to Tom and other people if he, Fred, does nothing about the situation. Yet if Fred does
get involved, there could be repercussions. "No matter what I do,"
Fred tells himself, "it's going to get ugly."

Hard Liquor and Hard Choices

To act with ethical intelligence often means doing something rather
than nothing when you're wondering, "What's the right thing to
do?" In this case, for example, ignoring the situation will allow a
serious, potentially life-threatening problem to continue. Fred, however, is in a position to promote change. Keeping in mind the Prevent Harm corollary to the first principle of ethical intelligence,

getting involved is the right thing for him to do. But what kind of involvement is called for? Talking with Tom about the issue may not help matters. After all, what is Tom likely to say? Most likely, one of the following things:

- "Oh, lighten up! It was a party! I was just having some fun."
- "Yes, I know I have a problem, but I'm taking steps to address it. Thank you for your concern."
- "I'm going through a tough time at home. Cut me some slack."
- "It's none of your business!"

Someone with a drinking problem usually can't solve it on his or her own, so it's misguided for him or her to say, "I can handle it." If Fred wants his intervention to be effective, he will have to contact the appropriate department at the company. This will probably be human resources.

No one likes to do this sort of thing. Fred would reasonably fear that if Tom finds out that Fred initiated an investigation into Tom's behavior, Tom might seek retribution. Many companies have antiretaliation policies, but reprisals can happen nevertheless. Tom might become angry with Fred. He might give Fred undesirable work. He might prevent Fred from getting a raise or a promotion, and in a worst-case scenario, he could find a way to fire Fred.

Then there is the sad reality that some attempts to get help for someone with an alcohol problem are met with indifference. I speak from experience. Many years ago, I took the keys away from someone who had had way too much to drink. A police officer who saw me doing this instructed me to give the woman her keys back and suggested that if I didn't, I would be arrested. I returned the keys under protest, got the officer's name, and called the sheriff the next day. The sheriff made light of the matter and said that he would not investigate it. Case closed.

There are thus several valid reasons for Fred to do nothing about Tom's drinking problem. Nevertheless, the ethically intelligent question for Fred to ask himself is this: "Is it better to take steps to prevent harm to my boss and others, even at the risk of alienating him or not being taken seriously, or keep it to myself and hope that someone else gets involved or that Tom solves the problem on his own?" It's true that Fred has an ethical obligation to himself to remain gainfully employed. It's also the case that if Fred does nothing, the following harms could occur:

- Tom's effectiveness as a senior manager could be compromised if he drinks on the job.
- Tom's health could continue to spiral downward.
- Tom could drive while intoxicated, collide with other drivers, and hurt or kill people, including himself.
- Tom could get drunk at a restaurant, be recognized by several patrons as a senior manager at the company, lose several potential clients, and damage the company's reputation.

Fred has good reasons to do nothing, but he has better reasons to take the appropriate measures to get help for Tom. Fred's dilemma presents a striking example of how difficult it can be to make ethically intelligent choices. It also suggests that finding some way to make those choices can prevent serious harm to a whole lot of people — and bring out the best in you, the person with the courage to make the tough choices.

I asked two experts in the field of substance abuse and treatment what their thoughts were on this case study. "The best outcomes occur when [human resources] departments insist on a professional evaluation rather than accuse the individual of having a drinking problem," said Dr. Omar Manejwala, medical director of Hazelden, one of the world's leading treatment centers for drug and alcohol addiction.[6] Dr. Manejwala added that Tom's situation is relatively common, and he cited a recent study by the National Survey on Drug Use and Health, which found that 8 percent of employed men and women have a substance abuse problem.[7]

Chuck Rice, a licensed alcohol and drug abuse counselor at Hazelden who is in recovery himself and uses his experience to help addicts,[8] told me how important it is for people in Fred's position to take action. "In my thirteen years of experience treating men with chemical dependency, the workplace is generally the last area of a man's life to be impacted by alcohol or drug use," Rice said. "By the time it starts to show up in the work environment, it is likely that the rest of his life is in shambles. Nothing will get an employed male into treatment faster than some form of workplace intervention or mandate. Often, the mere threat of such is sufficient."[9]

Both Dr. Manejwala and Chuck Rice emphasized that as unpleasant as an intervention can be for all concerned, it is quite possible for the addicted employee to be successfully treated and eventually return to work. But if no one else is willing to make the first move, Fred (and others in his position) will have to do so.

SUMMARY

Here are some ways to respond with ethical intelligence to boss-related issues.

Trash Talk

Offensive language after hours is merely offensive, but at work, it can damage relationships with clients, harm the company's reputation, strain working relationships, and call one's leadership ability into question. Just as your boss has a right to expect you to comport yourself professionally while you're on the job, you have a right to expect this of your boss. It's best to bring up your concerns directly rather than start with human resources or your boss's supervisor. If your boss persists in the uncouth behavior after you've raised the issue with him or her, the Prevent Harm corollary to the first principle of ethical intelligence calls upon you to take your concerns to the appropriate party.

Criticism

No one likes to be criticized, but ethically intelligent criticism helps you do your job better and perhaps grow as a person, too. Other varieties can be demoralizing and hurtful. Personal attacks, inappropriate displays of anger, and other forms of wrongful criticism are at odds with ethical intelligence, and as with the trash-talking boss, you have a right not to be subjected to such conduct. It's bullying, and you deserve better. But you'll have to speak up to get it to stop.

Objectionable Assignments

There are lots of reasons why you might object to an assignment. Merely finding the task distasteful or unpleasant doesn't justify a refusal. But if you're asked to do something that could harm you or others, could exploit clients, or involves committing other unethical acts, there are several ethically intelligent options: refusing to participate and finding creative ways of getting the job done in an ethical fashion are two noteworthy ones. Even if your job requires taking risks (such as removing asbestos or controlling pests), you have a right to have potential harms minimized.

The Boss with an Alcohol or Drug Problem

It's hard enough to intervene when someone close to you is wrestling with an addiction, but when the addict is your boss, you are forced to make one of the most difficult decisions you'll ever confront: do nothing, which is easier and more likely to keep your relationship intact, or contact the appropriate office or person in your organization, which may very well anger your boss if he or she finds out. Even with nonretaliation policies in place, we all know that people can find a way to get back at the whistleblower. But if you view an intervention not as punishment but as the most caring thing you can do for your boss and others who might be affected by your boss's behavior, then the answer is clear: you must intervene. The question is this: Can you find the courage to do it?

CHAPTER 8

Stand by Me

Ethical Intelligence with Your Clients, Shareholders, and Others with a Stake in Your Company

As I suggested earlier, business ethics in the traditional sense concerns what businesses owe to consumers. It is thus fitting to look at the responsibility to be honest about the products you sell and the services you offer; to provide excellent customer service; to inform stakeholders what's going on when the CEO takes a leave of absence; and to apologize when you have made a mistake. But as we saw when we analyzed the box-office dilemma in chapter 3, business ethics is also about what consumers owe to businesses. The customer isn't always right, and businesses not only have a right to stand up to unfair demands; they have an ethical obligation to do so. In this chapter, we'll look at business ethics in this broader sense — what businesses and customers owe to one another — by considering the following issues:

- The unethical customer
- The CEO taking a leave of absence
- Outsourcing customer service
- The ethics of "let the buyer beware"
- The ethics of apologies

I will use the term *stakeholder* in some contexts and *shareholder* in others. A stakeholder is anyone who has a stake in an organization, not necessarily a financial stake. Examples include, but are not limited to, employees, clients, and members of the board of directors or trustees. *Shareholder* is a term of more limited scope and refers only to those who own shares of stock in a public or private corporation. Generally speaking, shareholders are stakeholders, but not all stakeholders are shareholders.[1]

THE CUSTOMER ISN'T ALWAYS RIGHT

Frank, a restaurant manager, once told me about a customer named Tilly who ate most of her meal, complained that "it didn't taste right," and said she didn't think she should be charged for it. "It didn't feel right to go along with her, but my philosophy is that the customer is always right. Did I do the right thing?" Frank said. "One more thing: I know for a fact that Tilly isn't poor, which would have made the situation quite different."

Frank had no obligation to do what Tilly asked. In fact, doing so was wrong because it enabled Tilly to take advantage of the establishment. We've all gotten meals at restaurants that weren't to our liking, but the time to tell the server about it is after the first bite, not the thirtieth one. Giving Tilly a free meal simply because she asked for it wasn't fair to the other customers who paid for what they ate. The fourth principle of ethical intelligence, Be Fair, and its call to give others their due, is a crucial one in business ethics and applies not just to how businesses treat customers but (as I'll explore in more detail in chapter 9) how customers treat businesses, too. By getting something for nothing, Tilly wasn't being fair to Frank's establishment, and by giving her something for nothing, Frank wasn't being fair to the other customers, who eventually paid for their meals. The customer isn't always right, as this situation shows.

Business ethics is usually discussed in terms of the obligations that businesses owe to customers: manufacturing safe products, providing warranties on those products, honoring their advertisements, and the like. But businesses have rights as well as responsibilities, and foremost among them is the right not to be taken advantage of by their customers. By the same token, customers have responsibilities as well as rights. Tilly would rightfully be outraged if Frank advertised "Get a free dessert with the purchase of one entrée" but then declined to provide Tilly with a dessert because the campaign was costing the restaurant too much. "You promised a free dessert, so I expect you to stand by your promise," Tilly could reasonably say. Tilly is entitled to be treated justly by the restaurant, and the reverse is true as well.

The first principle of ethical intelligence, Do No Harm, is also implicated by this scenario. If Frank caves in to whatever customers want from him, even if what they're asking for is unfair, his restaurant's revenue will be diminished, perhaps significantly so. The irony is that Frank's attempt to please his customers — that is, to do something good — can actually cause harm to the business he represents if those customers take advantage of him. The notion that "it's nice to be important, but it's more important to be nice" has a limit: the Do No Harm principle.

Ethically Intelligent Responses to the Unethical Customer

Suppose that next week, a man named Ralph pulls the same stunt that Tilly did and that, like Tilly, Ralph is able to pay for his meal. Here is how Frank could rise to the occasion with ethical intelligence.

FRANK. So you say that the meal didn't taste very good?

RALPH. That's right, and I shouldn't have to pay for it.

FRANK, *looking perplexed.* Hmmm. Well, sir, please help me to understand why you didn't tell your server this after you had the first bite.[2]

RALPH. Are you calling me a liar?

FRANK. Not at all. It's just that you ate a lot of it, considering it didn't taste very good.

RALPH, *getting angry*. I figured I'd give the food a chance.

FRANK. It looks like you gave it many chances. Almost to the end, in fact.

RALPH. Are you saying you're going to make me pay for this lousy food? Haven't you ever heard that the customer is always right?

FRANK. Satisfying the customer is our first priority.

RALPH, *figuring he is getting his way*. Good.

FRANK. But there are limits to what we can do. You ate most of your meal, so it's only fair that you pay for it. But here's what I'll do. *(Ralph smiles and anticipates getting a certificate for a free dinner on his next visit.)* I'll be happy to give you a complimentary soda the next time you come for lunch or dinner.

RALPH. A free soda? That's all I get?

FRANK. I'd say that's more than fair.

RALPH. Well, I don't. I'm never coming back here again. *(Ralph reaches into his wallet and hastily pays the bill but doesn't include a tip for the server.)*

FRANK. I wish you all the best.

By sticking to his principles — the principles of ethical intelligence — Frank is losing a customer, so he obviously must choose wisely how often he will decide that the customer isn't right. But no matter what business you're in, you're entitled to be treated fairly by your clients. When a customer makes an unfair request, you not only have a right to refuse to honor it; you have an ethical obligation to do so.

WHEN THE CEO TAKES A LEAVE OF ABSENCE

On January 17, 2011, Apple cofounder and CEO Steve Jobs told employees that he would be taking a medical leave, his third in seven years. He didn't reveal any details about his illness but asked that his family's privacy, as well as his own, be respected.[3]

Was this an ethically intelligent request for Jobs to make? What would an ethically intelligent response for Apple's stakeholders be?

The Right to Privacy and the CEO

In chapter 2, I explained that the third principle of ethical intelligence, Respect Others, calls upon us to keep private things private. I suggested that the two physicians who discussed a patient's medical condition and mentioned the patient's full name in a hospital elevator had betrayed the patient's trust. Presumably that patient would not have wanted sensitive information about his medical condition discussed in front of people like me, and he was entitled to have his wish respected.

But not everyone has a right to have information about his or her health kept private. Some leadership roles require transparency because others have a right to know whether their leader is capable of doing the job at hand. For example, the president of the United States cannot legitimately claim a right to medical privacy; democracy requires that citizens be informed about their leader's health because health is a necessary condition for being able to protect their interests through this supremely demanding work. That the public has a right of access to the president's medical condition has been recognized only recently. Information about Grover Cleveland's surgery to remove an oral cancer, Woodrow Wilson's stroke, and Franklin D. Roosevelt's melanoma was kept from public view for fear that it would damage the president's political power, but this is now rightly regarded as something one expects in a totalitarian state, not a democracy.[4]

The CEO of a publicly traded company is to the company's stakeholders what the leader of a democratic society is to its citizens in at least one sense: both leadership positions entail restrictions on the leader's right to privacy. No one forces a person to take the helm of a public company or a country; one does so with the understanding that the job requires a degree of transparency that doesn't apply to most other people. Stakeholders and citizens alike are entitled to know what is going on with the person they chose to lead them. When this person falls ill, he or she ought to disclose his or her current medical condition and prognosis, the treatment options, and how well he or she is doing as this ordeal progresses. Thus the ethically intelligent thing for Jobs to have done when announcing his medical leave would have been to explain the nature of his illness (while rightfully expecting stakeholders to leave his family alone).

Some worry about the financial implications for the company that such a disclosure would have. But in the long run, the organization is likely to benefit, not lose, financially because it's the lack of information that causes investors to express concern about the company's future and downgrade its stock valuation. If ever there was a situation that illustrates the old saw "Knowledge is power," it is this one.

Just as a CEO of a public company who needs to take medical leave has responsibilities toward stakeholders, stakeholders have responsibilities toward the CEO. Compassion, an aspect of the fifth principle of ethical intelligence, is high on this list. When a CEO announces that he or she has a serious illness, stakeholders ought to be concerned not just about the company but about its leader as well. Recall from chapter 6 that *compassion* literally means "to suffer with."

This discussion highlights the need for every company to have a succession plan in place. After all, nothing lasts forever, so the prudent thing for any leader to do before he or she becomes ill is to anoint the next in line. No one likes to confront the reality that we're not going to live forever, but the ethically intelligent CEO does so anyway.

OUTSOURCING CUSTOMER SERVICE

It was a dark and stormy night, and I was having major problems with my desktop computer. Having anticipated this moment, I had purchased an extended warranty plan, and I called the manufacturer's customer service phone number, assuming that I'd be given prompt attention.

"Hello, my name is Steve," a crackly, faraway voice said on the other end of the line. It sounded as if he were underwater. "Maybe the service center is in Atlantis," I reasoned, and proceeded apace with my concerns. "Hi Steve. My computer isn't booting up, and I don't know what to do."

Steve asked me to check something, but because of his thick accent, I couldn't understand what he was referring to. I asked him to repeat himself, which he did, but I still couldn't make heads or tails of it. Even with two more tries, I was unable to comprehend what Steve wanted me to do.

"I'm sorry, Steve, but I simply can't understand what you're saying," I said with frustration. I knew that he wasn't in the United States, so I asked him if he could please transfer me to an associate who was. He politely said he would, but I was then put on hold for over twenty minutes while some insipid advertisement for the company played over and over. I hung up the phone, thirty minutes older than I was when I placed the call but no closer to a solution.

I called the toll-free number again and got someone named Mary, but it was close to impossible to understand her as well. It was clear that I'd have to hire someone at my own expense to fix my computer. It was also clear that I'd never again buy another computer from this company, which I'll refer to here as the World's Worst Customer Service Company Inc., or World's Worst for short.

The leadership of World's Worst apparently thought it would save money by outsourcing its customer service overseas. In the short run, it may very well have done that; by slashing labor costs, it enriched the bottom line and kept shareholders happy. But in the long run, outsourcing customer service is both bad for business and ethically unintelligent. In fact, it's bad for business *because* it is ethically unintelligent.

Good Word of Mouth and How Not to Get It

The most valuable commodity a business has, and the most difficult one to come by, is positive word of mouth. There are lots of ways to engender this. You can build a superior product. You can create a memorable marketing campaign. You can get publicity by doing good works in the community. All of these will inevitably get people talking about your company, which is harder and harder to make happen in our increasingly crowded marketplace.

The problem with outsourcing customer service is that this practice creates what Jed Clampett would call "a whole heap" of negative word of mouth. Time is precious, and who wants to spend an inordinate amount of time in an often vain attempt to communicate with a company employee who is halfway around the world and cannot speak English effectively? My experience with Steve was not the first one (or second, or even third) that I had with World's Worst, and you can be sure that I have warned my wide circle of friends and associates to avoid this company at all costs. In telling my friends about my horrible experiences, I discovered that — not surprisingly — I'm far from the only customer disgruntled by the customer service provided by World's Worst. One can only imagine how much business the company has lost by valuing short-term financial gain over standing by the people who buy their products. World's Worst has a formidable task ahead of it because it's harder to repair a poor reputation than it is to create and maintain a good one in the first place.

Smart businesses recognize that the surest way to hold on to their current customers and create new ones is to place customer satisfaction front and center, not only in their mission statements but in their day-to-day operations. This means that customer service representatives must be able to communicate clearly. This also means that these employees should be fluent not only in the primary language of the customer base but in their culture, customs, and idiosyncrasies as well. The root of *customer* is *custom*, and customs are largely a mystery to those who live and work outside of the culture concerned.

Is This a Racist Proposal?

To criticize the practice of outsourcing customer service may seem racist. After all, the people who have those outsourced jobs are largely people of color whose first language is not English. Isn't this proposal a thinly veiled discrimination against non-U.S. cultures?

No, it isn't. The reason it is wrong for U.S. businesses to give customer service jobs to non–native speakers of English who live overseas has nothing to do with race. My argument here isn't even against outsourcing as such. That is, even if one believes that businesses have an obligation to minimize labor costs, it doesn't follow that customer service positions are best suited to contractors from other countries.[5] These jobs require being able to communicate well. As anyone can attest who has had a poor customer service experience with residents of Bangalore, Manila, and other cities where U.S. outsourcing is popular, company representatives there for the most part are not measuring up, so they ought not to have jobs where being intelligible in English, the primary language of a company's customers, is essential.

The key word in the above conclusion is *intelligible*, not *intelligent*. This analysis should not be interpreted as a slight against the intelligence or integrity of non-U.S. citizens. Nor do I mean to suggest that residents of the above cities do not do good work. I'm merely observing that it can be difficult to understand what someone who isn't a native speaker of English is saying. This can be the case even with some Americans who are native English speakers but who may lack communication skills or have especially heavy regional accents. They're not candidates for customer service jobs either, for the same reason. Also, my argument against outsourcing isn't limited to interactions between U.S.-based customers and business representatives located in other countries. Conversational challenges exist between peoples of any two countries or regions in which the primary languages are different from one another.

Adding to the intelligibility issue is the fact that the phone connection to people in distant lands is often substandard, as my experience with Steve showed (and I'll bet this has happened to you as well). Outsourced customer service thus presents two major obstacles to effective communication: a language barrier and a technological challenge. These obstacles strain and, in some cases, damage relationships with the very people a business purports to serve, so outsourced customer service runs counter to the first principle of ethical intelligence, Do No Harm, as well as the third principle, Respect Others. It subverts two crucial objectives in business: to understand the needs of customers and to meet those needs effectively. If enough customers become disgruntled, their negative word of mouth is likely to impede profits, which prevents the company from fulfilling the second principle of ethical intelligence, Make Things Better, for its stakeholders.

It is ironic, then, that a for-profit organization would choose to engage in a practice that subverts its very mission: to make a profit. The problem isn't the mission itself. After all, a business isn't a charity. Where too many businesses falter, though, is leaping from the premise "Money is good" to the conclusion "We ought to do anything legal that will maximize profits." This leap of logic is ethically troublesome since much wrongful behavior is legally permissible.

Furthermore, the obsession with making the most money, and doing so sooner rather than later, blinds one to the very thing that promotes a flourishing business in the first place: satisfied customers who keep coming back for more. A business will not and cannot succeed if it puts greater emphasis on short-term gain than on customer satisfaction.

Corporate officers should explain to shareholders that the smart business is one that values meeting the needs of customers above all else, including short-term financial gain. Only by having its priorities straight can a company count on long-term financial gain. The goals of making a profit and satisfying customers are not mutually exclusive. Just the opposite is true: these two goals are inextricably bound together.

Here, then, is a challenge to your own company: put a premium on serving the needs of customers by keeping customer service jobs in this country. You'll make your clientele happy, generate positive word of mouth, enrich our own economy, and, in the long run, enjoy continued growth and success. Your customers (and shareholders) will thank you for it.

Keeping customer service jobs at home, rather than sending them abroad, is the ethically intelligent thing to do for any business that wants to be in business for a long, long time.

IS "LET THE BUYER BEWARE" ETHICALLY INTELLIGENT?

When I was ten, I bought some gizmo that turned out to be a piece of junk.

"Caveat emptor!" my mom told me when I showed her the busted toy I'd just spent my hard-earned allowance on.

"What does that mean?" I asked.

"Let the buyer beware," she said. "You can't believe everything people tell you when they want to sell you something."

I know I'm not the only one who has thrown away cash because of inaccurate advertising. The list of false or deceptive claims made about goods and services is as long as forty miles of bad road and just as perilous. Thus it has made sense for consumers to do their due diligence before buying something even as relatively inexpensive as a microwave oven or dinner for two at a local restaurant.

But caveat emptor is a poor business philosophy because it is ethically unintelligent.

Profits over People?

Traditionally, the business-customer relationship was distinguished from the one between physicians and patients or that between lawyers and clients, in that customers were assumed to have the wherewithal to assess the claims that businesses made about their products and services. The burden of proof for assessing the validity of these claims therefore sat on the shoulders of consumers. Even before reviews became readily available on the Internet, buyers were theoretically in a position to decide whether a vacuum cleaner, a piece of furniture, or a stereo was all that its seller said it was.

This sort of detective work was not (and, to some degree, still is not) considered possible in health care or law. How can patients reasonably decide whether the antibiotic or antidepressant their doctors recommend is safe and effective? If you need to understand a complex contract, how can you expect to do this effectively if you haven't had specialized training in the relevant law? We trust health-care providers, attorneys, and other professionals not only to possess expertise that we don't but also to be concerned primarily with our best interests, not their own. As long as they honor this trust, it makes sense for professions to be less regulated than business is. After all, the main objective of business is to make a profit, not to benefit the public, right?

This question presumes that there is an inherent conflict between making money and helping others. But it doesn't require an MBA to see that the Great Recession grew out of the false belief that not only does prosperity involve placing profits ahead of people — but it also requires this. For example, lenders who gave subprime mortgages to people at a high risk of default didn't care that the loans wouldn't be repaid. They knew they would make a nice profit when these loans were packaged and sold to Wall Street right after closing, and that's exactly what happened. Their short-term gains resulted in long-term losses for you and me, and many of the businesses involved in this shell game have tanked. Making money without regard to how the money was made turned out to be both unethical and bad for business.

In a postrecession world, successful managers and entrepreneurs will be men and women of conscience who understand that profitability depends upon building and maintaining trust with the public. The secret to reclaiming this trust lies in something that hasn't been a staple of business practice: telling consumers the truth. Let's look at a recent example of how false, misleading, or unsubstantiated claims have hurt one important business sector and why it no longer makes financial sense to regard the truth — and, by implication, the well-being of the public — in such a cavalier fashion.

The Truth, but Not the Whole Truth

In 2010, the U.S. Food and Drug Administration warned several companies against making false or misleading claims about their products.[6] A juice manufacturer stated on its website that its product could work wonders for high blood pressure, clogged arteries, and even prostate cancer. Such claims, if true, would certainly qualify the beverage as a miracle drug, but there is no evidence that such a cause-and-effect relationship exists. Another company, on the packaging for one of its ice cream confections, stated that its product had zero grams of trans fat per serving. That statement is true, but the confection also has twenty grams of saturated fat per serving. No one would rationally consider ice cream to be a health food, but this company's partial truth could mislead people into thinking that this treat is healthier than it is.

The full, unvarnished truth has been treated with such indifference by many in the business community for so long that taking advertisements at face value is ridiculous. But this is why it's no longer feasible for businesses, whatever sector they're in, to trade in less than the truth. Treating consumers with respect, which means, in part, telling them the truth, is the only way companies can hope to turn a cynical public around and restore their faith in commerce. Remember Warren Beatty's film *Bulworth*? It suggested that telling the truth in politics was the stuff of comedy and satire. But honesty is no laughing matter in government or business.

Truth Telling: The Smart Business Move

Why are business executives, advertising professionals, and car salespeople consistently at or near the bottom of Gallup's annual Honesty and Ethics survey?[7] It's not because business is an inherently ignoble calling; it's because too many people in its ranks consider high ethical standards (or any ethical standards at all) to be unnecessary or even liabilities.[8]

The smart manager, however, can no longer afford to think this way. The companies that prosper in our postrecession economy will be the ones committed to being forthright about what they sell. They will view truthfulness and other elements of ethical intelligence not as burdens that must be accepted reluctantly but as the key to building and maintaining relationships with customers and ultimately enriching the bottom line. Doing right by your customers is the best way for you to do right by your business and its stakeholders.

It's time to retire caveat emptor — "let the buyer beware." The new motto in business should be *vincit omnia veritas* — "truth conquers all."

SORRY SEEMS TO BE THE HARDEST WORD: WHAT IS AN ETHICALLY INTELLIGENT APOLOGY?

A running gag in the 1970s sitcom *Happy Days* was Arthur "Fonzie" Fonzarelli's inability to admit a mistake. The first two words, "I was," came out fine, but it was that third one, "wrong," that always tripped him up. Try as he might (and boy, did he try), the Fonz simply could not proclaim error. "I was wrrrr-rrr-rrr——" was about the closest he could get. Decades later, many of us are still laughing at how Fonzie exemplified this all-too-human foible.

We've seen that it's hard to accept constructive criticism, but the ethically intelligent thing is to somehow find a way to do just that. We've also recognized that it can be difficult to resist an attraction to a coworker, but acting on that attraction is generally not consistent with ethical intelligence. As the Fonz reminds us, having the courage to admit we've screwed up is one of the hardest things to do. It's also one of the most important.

How Not to Apologize

We'll examine the ethically intelligent apology by going through the back door, so to speak. Here are some examples of the wrong way to apologize, along with an explanation of how they contradict the principles of ethical intelligence.

1. *Say, "Mistakes were made."* This classic dodge is a favorite of business leaders and politicians alike. Although its use in government isn't limited to one political party, the phrase is most famously associated with Ronald Reagan's 1987 State of the Union address, in which the president used it to refer to the Iran-Contra scandal.

"Mistakes were made" is rightly referred to as a "nonapology apology" because this phrase is in the passive voice and thereby absolves the speaker of any responsibility. Its use by a leader is ethically unintelligent because a critical component of leadership is accountability. Stating that "mistakes were made" is simply another way of saying, "Bad things happened on my watch. But other people did them, and I can't be blamed."

2. *Change the subject.* Refusing to address a problem one has caused makes psychological sense. After all, who wants to admit that he or she is flawed in some way? Those who feel that admitting error is a sign of weakness are likely to change the subject when confronted with mistakes they made. It's not an ethically intelligent move, however, because it fails to acknowledge the reality that we are, in fact, less than perfect. Recall that one way to apply the third principle of ethical intelligence, Respect Others, is to tell the truth to those who have a right to know it. A leader shows respect to the people he or she is leading by informing them of things they need to know, which often (but not always) includes an acknowledgment that the leader has erred in some way.

3. *Drag your feet.* Remember when U.S. Department of Agriculture official Shirley Sherrod was abruptly fired after Andrew Breitbart circulated an edited video of Sherrod that made her appear racist? Agriculture Secretary Tom Vilsack eventually apologized to Sherrod and took full responsibility for having exercised poor judgment by dismissing her.[9] Sherrod accepted the apology and said that it made her feel better. But she also stated that it "took too long" to come, and she ultimately chose not to accept the White House's offer to be reinstated.[10] Vilsack deserves credit for owning up to his serious mistake and attempting to right a wrong that he had committed, but for the person on the receiving end of the injustice, he should have done this sooner.[11]

The fourth principle of ethical intelligence, Be Fair, has a temporal component. It's not enough to give someone his or her due; one must do so in time.

4. *Deny there is a problem.* Burying your head in the sand in response to a blunder is ethically unintelligent because there is such a thing as reality. Your mistake is still a mistake, whether or not you're able to accept this fact. Both it and the consequences that followed from it occurred, whether or not you want to believe this is true.

5. *Admit that you did* x, *but claim that* x *isn't wrong.* When someone accuses you of having done something wrong, and you believe what you did was right, you should be prepared to back up your actions with a rational argument. Ethical intelligence involves more than doing the right thing; it also requires justifying — that is, providing good reasons for — the choices one makes. Reasonable people can disagree about many things, including the rightness or wrongness of some forms of conduct.

But certain actions, such as theft, fraud, and assault, cannot be defended from an ethical point of view. Imagine that your financial adviser took the money you gave her to invest for you and used it instead to pay for her son's college education. When you discover this and confront her with the evidence, she replies, "Yes, I lied to you and took your money without your knowledge or consent. You may think this is wrong, but I think it's right because without this money, my son couldn't have afforded to continue his education." Presumably, your reaction wouldn't be to say, "Well, we just have a different opinion about whether lying and stealing are right or wrong." You would believe — correctly so — that there is such a thing as right and wrong, and that being a liar and a thief is in the second category, no matter who is considering the issue or what arguments are marshaled in their defense.[12]

Some things are ethical, some things are not, and it's wrong-headed to believe otherwise. Your thief of a financial adviser isn't so much making a legitimate defense of her actions as she is refusing to accept responsibility for what she did, apologize, and make the appropriate reparations.

6. *Blame someone else.* The worst oil spill in history started when the *Deepwater Horizon* rig exploded in the Gulf of Mexico. Although the rig was licensed by BP, the company's CEO, Tony Hayward, initially had this to say about his company's accountability: "The responsibility for safety on the drilling rig is Transocean [*sic*]. It is their rig, their equipment, their people, their systems, their safety processes."[13] BP eventually accepted the blame for the catastrophe, but not before a mountain of evidence made it impossible for them to deny their culpability. For years to come, this will no doubt be the ultimate gold standard for how not to apologize for one's mistakes.

How to Apologize with Ethical Intelligence

The fourth principle of ethical intelligence, Be Fair, calls upon us to give others their due. When you mess up in some way, fairness requires an apology. However, some forms of wrongful conduct are so serious that a mere "I'm sorry" isn't enough of a response. With this in mind, here are some guidelines for making ethically intelligent apologies.

1. *Admit your mistake quickly and take personal responsibility for it.* Don't say "We made a mistake" when you mean "I made a mistake." Even if you're not the head of your organization, the buck should still stop with you.

2. *Apologize first to the person you have wronged.* That is the person who matters most.

3. *Speak from the heart.* An insincere apology is as bad as no apology at all. People can tell when you really mean it, even if you think you're a good actor and can fool everyone. If you truly believe

you're not in the wrong, don't apologize — but be prepared to defend your position.

4. *Realize that sorry is just a word.* For that word to be meaningful, you must do your level best to avoid repeating the mistake. This means coming up with a strategy and sticking to it.

5. *Know that a meaningful apology is a sign of integrity, not weakness.* Anyone can blame others, or deny that he or she did anything wrong, or lie about what really happened. Only a strong, self-possessed person can own up to his or her mistakes, and only such a person commands true respect.

6. *Don't be afraid to ask for help.* If you can't do something well on your own, invite others to work with you on the problem. If the problem is beyond your grasp, consider asking someone else to take it on, if it is appropriate for you to do so.

How to *Respond* to Apologies with Ethical Intelligence

When you're on the receiving end of an apology, it's useful to keep the fifth principle of ethical intelligence, Be Loving, in mind (and heart). Ethically intelligent people do what they can to honor a person's sincere apology, even though their anger pulls them in the opposite direction. The following guidelines present ethically intelligent ways of responding to apologies.

- If someone has done something wrong and apologizes to you, accept the apology graciously. (However, bear in mind the other points in this list.)
- You are justified in expecting a person to avoid repeating the behavior that required an apology in the first place.
- Depending on the situation, you might need to make clear to the other person what the consequences will be if he or she makes the mistake again.

- "Three strikes and you're out" is fine for baseball, but in other areas, it may take only one strike for someone to be justifiably banished from being a player. Some mistakes are so serious that you should not grant a second chance. For relatively minor errors, however, or if the task at hand is unusually difficult, it might be unfair not to allow more than three opportunities to get it right.

- If the person who apologized continues making the same mistake over and over, you may have to say, perhaps regrettably, "I can't in good conscience give you another opportunity to slip up," no matter how much that person continues to apologize.

The 1970 film *Love Story* featured the memorable, if perplexing, line "Love means never having to say you're sorry." Even if this were true, there are many other areas where we do have to say we're sorry — and mean it. The challenge for all of us is to admit we've made a mistake, to do our best to ensure we don't do it again, and to forgive others who sincerely regret their own poor judgment. No one is perfect, but most of us do have the capacity to right our own wrongs and to accept the imperfections of others.

SUMMARY

Five areas in the business/stakeholder relationship can — but don't have to — compromise one's ethical intelligence.

The Unethical Customer

Just as managers and others in business have an obligation not to take advantage of customers, they also have a right not be taken advantage of by customers. Exercising this right may result in some lost business, but the ethically intelligent response to this is, "Goodbye and good riddance!"

The CEO Taking a Leave of Absence

It is ethically intelligent for a CEO who must take a medical leave of absence to explain to stakeholders why he or she is doing so. Both the third and fourth principles of ethical intelligence — Respect Others and Be Fair — require this response. Stakeholders should remember that the fifth principle, Be Loving, calls upon them to be compassionate at times like this.

Outsourcing Customer Service

Because of the potential for poor communication, which can lead to disgruntled customers choosing to take their business elsewhere, the practice of outsourcing customer service is inconsistent with ethical intelligence. A business's obsessive focus on short-term financial gain can be damaging in the long run to its relationships with customers and shareholders alike.

The Ethics of "Let the Buyer Beware"

"Let the buyer beware" is an ethically unintelligent way to do business because by being forthright about what customers can expect from their goods and services, businesses are more likely to engender trust, promote positive word of mouth, and do well by everyone with a stake in the company.

The Ethics of Apologies

Apologizing with ethical intelligence means admitting to, and taking responsibility for, the mistakes one has made, asking for forgiveness, and making the necessary reparations. Those who have been wronged have a right to expect that the wrongdoer will not repeat his or her mistake. Accepting an apology graciously is a compassionate thing to do, and forgiveness makes it easier (if not easy) to move on. Bitterness hurts only the person feeling it.

PART 3

Ethical Intelligence in Your Personal Life

CHAPTER 9

We Are Family

Ethical Intelligence with Your Family, Friends, and Community

The closer someone is to you, the harder it is to think straight when relationship problems, and the ethical issues they include, arise. Let's see what the principles of ethical intelligence have to say about:

- Work-life balance
- Being a tightwad
- Taking vacations
- Relationships with local businesses

GET RICH OR DIE TRYIN': THE ETHICALLY INTELLIGENT WORK-LIFE BALANCE

My friend Joanne's grandfather Charlie prided himself on never having missed a day on the job. He had grown up in poverty and wanted to make sure that his family was provided for in a way that he himself had not been. The upside was that his family, which included Joanne's dad, Brian, had a comfortable place to live, plenty to eat, and new clothes when they needed them. The downside is that Charlie missed all of his six children's high school graduations. He never attended any of the kids' baseball games, choral concerts, or swim meets. His son Brian grew up without seeing his dad very much.

Not surprisingly, Brian adopted the same work ethic, but with a twist: he did take time off for his two kids, but work was always involved in some way. Brian was the head of the PTA, a deacon of the church, and the coach of Joanne's softball team. Late every evening, after a busy day at his job and various community activities, Brian would plop himself down on the couch to watch TV — and promptly fall asleep. Joanne's memories of her father, now deceased, are usually associated with work of some kind. She loved her father dearly but wondered what he would have been like away from the many jobs he undertook. "I'm grateful for all he did for my brother and me," Joanne told me recently, "but I wish we had just 'hung out' once in awhile. I would have liked that, but it's too late now."

No issue presents a greater challenge to your ethical intelligence than what is referred to as "work-life balance." The way you approach it determines not only the quality of your life but also the quality of the relationships you have with *your* family, friends, and community. Work-life balance is an ethical issue because the fourth principle of ethical intelligence, Be Fair, calls upon you to give others their due, and one of the things you owe to others (and yourself) is your time. In fact, as I suggested in chapter 2, your time is the single most valuable resource you have because everything you do is based on its availability. It is also irreplaceable; once you've spent it, it's gone for good. How you allocate your time between your career and everything else speaks volumes about your commitment to fairness. It shows how ethically intelligent you are with respect to every important relationship you have.

Before we consider what an ethically intelligent balance between work and life might be, I should say that I don't like the phrase "work-life balance." It suggests that you have your career on the one hand and everything else on the other, but work is a part of life, not apart from it. Still, this is the term used in business journalism, so to be consistent, I will use it, under mild protest.

There are several reasons why our lives are so out of balance:

- Economic pressure
- Ready access to work
- Overvaluing our careers

Let's consider how to approach each one with ethical intelligence so that you can have a healthy balance between your work and everything else in your life.

Economic Pressure

According to a 2011 Gallup Poll, Americans worry more about money than we do about anything else, including job security, health care, and war.[1] We're still reeling from the recent financial crisis: pensions have been eliminated, portfolios have diminished in value, and savings accounts are being tapped for day-to-day expenses. In light of our shaky economic future, it makes sense that we have so much anxiety about our income. It's even worse, of course, for those who have lost their jobs in the wake of unprecedented nationwide job cuts. From December 2007 (the beginning of the Great Recession) until February 2010, 8.7 million jobs were lost in the United States.[2] In his book *How Starbucks Saved My Life*, Michael Gates Gill tells of his lucrative business going under and having to work at the coffee chain to get by.[3] People like Gill have had to work twice as hard to make half as much as they used to (or less). These folks aren't working seventy hours a week because they want to; they're doing it because they have to.

But it's one thing to have to work two jobs just to be able to put food on the table and pay the rent or mortgage. It's another to work so much to be able to afford lavish trips, expensive clothes, or a certain lifestyle. Instead of working longer, couldn't you shift your priorities so that you're able to spend more time with family and friends, exercise more often, or even just read some of those books you've been thinking about? In other words, there are several possible responses to the economic downturn: work more hours to be able to maintain one's standard of living or get an even higher one; or work the same number of hours, or even fewer, and place a greater emphasis on the most valuable thing that money can't buy — time with the people you care about.

Try this exercise: Write your obituary. Start with a headline that summarizes your main achievement in life and includes how old you'll be when you die. The first paragraph expands on the headline and includes where and how you'll die. The body of the obituary presents the highlights of your life in chronological order. The final paragraph or two describes something you did or said that captures your essence.

It sounds like a morbid thing to do, and no one wants to confront the reality that our lives have a beginning, a middle, and an end. But this exercise will help you see the narrative arc of your life. Knowing how you'd like to be remembered can prompt you to reexamine your work-life balance and, if necessary, make some changes for the better.

Ready Access to Work

Gone are the days when leaving your office meant leaving work behind. Many of us choose (or are expected) to use our BlackBerrys, iPhones, laptops, and social networking to remain constantly available to our bosses, clients, and colleagues, but this can get out of control. It's flattering to believe that you're indispensable to your company and that only you can do the work you spend so much time doing. But this is rarely true, however painful that may be to accept. Be honest with yourself: Are you spending so much time on the job because you must or because of habit, ego, or some other reason? You owe it to yourself and the people you care about to work smarter, not harder, which means unplugging from the Internet and cell phone every day and focusing on friends, family, and your own body, soul, and spirit.

But what if your boss expects you to be constantly available? This is ethically unintelligent management. Even professions such as health care, which require round-the-clock availability, do not and cannot expect their practitioners to be on call all day, every day. Would you want the physician caring for you in the hospital to make decisions about your care if he or she has not slept in thirty-six hours? For a long time, medical residents were required to submit to a punishing schedule that made restorative sleep hard to come by. But then a young woman named Libby Zion died in a New York hospital, and it became known that one of the residents caring for her was exhausted from overwork. Following this tragedy, the brutal schedule for residents was modified to preclude their having to work more than eighty hours a week averaged over a four-week period. It is also no longer permissible for residents to have shifts that last for a day and a half straight.[4] Whether or not you're a physician or nurse, and whether or not there are immediate life-or-death consequences to your being always on call, it is unfair for your employer to expect you to be accessible all the time.

When people I know complain about having to respond to every work-related email or phone call they get after hours, I ask them, "Have you told your boss you need some time away from work each day?" The answer is always the same: "No, I haven't." I appreciate how difficult it can be to stand up to one's supervisor, but there is an immutable law of human nature worth keeping in mind: if someone can take advantage of you, he or she probably will.

Eleanor Roosevelt once said, "No one can make you feel inferior without your consent." By the same token, no one can expect you to work around the clock without your consent. You have a right to time off, and it is up to you to have that right respected.[5]

Overvaluing Our Careers

I can't wait to get to work each day, and I usually have to force myself to stop to do other worthwhile things such as eat and sleep. There's no better feeling than writing something I'm happy with, giving a talk that connects with people, or doing a lively interview on TV or radio about things that matter. I can hardly believe I get paid to fly around the world to talk with folks about ethics. My career is a dream come true.

But there should be limits to even the most exciting career. Jack Torrance, the main character in the film *The Shining*, was right when he wrote, "All work and no play makes Jack a dull boy." (True, he was a murderous lunatic who wrote this sentence thousands of times, but the idea is still valid.) It's great to have a career that one is passionate about and to view one's job not merely as a means to a paycheck but as a calling. Yet it's wrong to define oneself exclusively by one's career. Even if what you do for a living is the most important thing to you, is it the only thing that's valuable? If not, giving an undue amount of your time and energy to your work is unfair. It deprives those other areas of your life — family, friends, community activities, hobbies — of something priceless and irreplaceable: you. In the context of work-life balance, giving others their due means allocating the right amount of time to your job and the right amount of time to the other things that make life worth living.

Life-Life Balance

Even when you're willing and able to put aside work in favor of the other things that life has to offer, another ethical question presents itself: Since you're not able to give all your time to everyone who may want or need it, on what basis should you allocate your time and energy? Generally speaking, the closer someone is to you, the greater claim that person has on your time. All things being equal, it's more important to spend time with your spouse or children than with a distant relative or even a good friend.

But this isn't always the case. Suppose a dear friend from your past with whom you have lost contact finds you on Facebook and says he's going to be in town in a few days. It wouldn't be unfair to set aside time for him, even if this means not being able to spend as much time alone with your family as you had been planning to. (By the same token, it wouldn't be unfair to say that you've already made plans; you can always catch up on the phone or the next time he's in the area.) All bets are off, however, when a former flame appears out of the blue. You may have been extremely close to this person way back when, but times have changed, and with it, your responsibilities.

It's not possible to be all things to all people at all times, and you have no reason to feel guilty for allocating your time with ethical intelligence.

A Time for Imbalance

Of course, there are times when it is ethically intelligent to let the work-life balance tilt in favor of work. As you approach an important deadline for your job, you may have to temporarily give a substantial amount of your time and energy to getting the job done at the expense of a healthy personal life. If, for example, one is writing a book on ethical intelligence that includes a section on work-life balance, one might have to sacrifice one's sanity for a limited period to meet one's professional standards and a tight production schedule. Cathexis — obsessive focus on a goal — is ethically justified in these limited circumstances. But that work-life seesaw shouldn't slope steeply to one side for too long.

Bottom line: You have a career; it shouldn't have you.

WHEN IS IT ETHICALLY INTELLIGENT TO BE A TIGHTWAD, AND WHEN IS IT JUST PLAIN CHEAP?

It's especially tough to make a living these days, so more than ever, spending our money carefully makes good sense. But cost-cutting measures that compromise other important values, such as honoring important relationships, are not ethically intelligent. Let's consider two different approaches to frugality; one of them is consistent with the principles of ethical intelligence, and one is not.

Parsimonious Polly

Polly works hard for her money and guards it very closely. She is vice president of communications of a small bank, and other than the mortgage on her modest home, she is proud that she has no outstanding debts of any kind. Most of Polly's friends have the same financial profile, but Polly is known to go to extreme lengths to save a buck. She'll drive ten miles out of her way to avoid a fifty-cent toll. She wraps presents in cheap aluminum foil to save on wrapping paper. Those presents — scented toiletries, dried fruit, overstock books — are bought in bulk once a year so she doesn't have to take the time to shop when birthdays and holidays roll around. Almost every conversation with her inevitably includes a reference to her latest cost-saving measures, each of which she considers a personal victory.

Some of Polly's friends and family members call her "Parsimonious Polly" because her reluctance to spend money has caused problems in their relationships with her. For example, Polly's Christmas gift to her cousin Bert was the book *Deep-Sea Diving in the Caribbean*. "Uh, thanks," Bert muttered when he peeled away the thin metallic wrapping from the book. Not only does Bert have no interest in oceanography, but Polly gave the same gift last Christmas (a book that Bert sees from time to time in the dusty remainder bins at his local bookstore). Polly's other present is a bag of dried apples and banana chips, neither of which Bert likes. Bert feels that Polly doesn't care about him and is merely satisfying an obligation to get him something, anything, during the holidays that will involve the least effort and expense possible. Yet Bert goes to some lengths to get Polly things he knows she'll like (based on the wish list Polly emails to her family and friends each November). Bert knows that Polly has positive qualities, but as far as he is concerned, her cheapness overrides those qualities; and he has developed a strong resentment toward his cousin.

Frugal Frieda

Like Polly, Frieda is careful with her money, but for different reasons and to different ends. Earlier this year, Frieda lost her job as an accountant for a local auto supply company, and she has not been able to find any work since then. She was even turned down for waitressing and entry-level salesclerk positions. Her unemployment benefits have run out, and she doesn't know how she'll pay for the health insurance she needs. With such a bleak financial future, Frieda isn't able to buy Christmas presents for her family and friends. Instead, she makes plates of her much-loved zesty lemon bars and oatmeal-walnut-chocolate-chip cookies; volunteers to babysit for her best friend, a single mom; and writes (by hand) heartfelt letters to everyone she knows, in which she expresses how grateful she is for the love she feels from them. She also feels compelled to apologize for not being able to buy any presents this year and explains why.

"You have nothing to apologize for," her friend Betty tells her after she receives Frieda's letter. "You haven't done anything wrong."

"I know, Betty, but I still feel ashamed. I love buying presents for the people I care about, and I thought about using my credit cards, but ———."

"There's no reason to run up debt you can't pay for," Betty interrupts. She can hear the sorrow in Frieda's voice, and it makes her sad. "Why make matters worse?"

Frieda appreciates what Betty says but still feels bad.

"Besides," Betty adds, "do you know how many handwritten letters I got all year? One. It was yours, and it was beautiful."

Frieda's eyes well with tears, partly because of her dire financial situation and partly because she is grateful for having a friend like Betty.

To Save or Spend?

At first blush, Polly's and Frieda's relationship to money appears to have nothing to do with ethics. Each woman's story raises psychological questions: What in Polly's background might have led her to become such a tightwad? What is her motivation — to unconsciously push people away or simply to save money for an early retirement? How will Frieda cope with the stress of her situation? But each woman's choices concern how a valuable resource is allocated, and the result of that decision affects their relationships, for better or worse. Once we start thinking about whether a person's actions are beneficial or harmful, and whether that person is allocating a valuable resource appropriately, we are smack-dab in the middle of ethical inquiry. I'll explain why Frieda's approach to personal finance is ethically intelligent but Polly's is not.

Polly *could* spend money on birthday and holiday presents, but she chooses not to. Even if we discovered the root causes of her parsimony, this would explain her behavior but not justify it. Suppose, for example, that Polly's parents didn't give her enough love and attention when she was young, and clinging to money is her way of coping with her fear of abandonment. Suppose also that Polly is indeed planning to retire within ten years and is saving as much as she can so that she'll be able to enjoy the rest of her life in style. Polly still has free will, and she makes decisions based on her own goals, preferences, and values. Her choices are hurtful to the people she presumably cares about and compromise the responsibility we all have to not damage relationships (per the first principle of ethical intelligence). Polly is so focused on saving money that when it comes time to give a family member or friend a gift, her only concern is how little money she can spend to get the job done. It matters very little to her, if at all, that her gifts are unwelcome or off-putting. Her way of celebrating holidays isn't caring or kind and thus fails to honor the fifth principle of ethical intelligence. Polly isn't an evil person, and she has positive qualities about her. But her relationship to money isn't ethically intelligent.

Frieda, on the other hand, *can't* spend money on presents without making her precarious financial situation worse. Ethics concerns not only how we treat others but also how we treat ourselves, and, as Frieda's friend Betty notes, running up credit card debt just to do some holiday shopping would be harmful to her. It would also compromise Frieda's ability to keep her promises since she might not be able to pay her creditors back anytime soon. Besides, Frieda has found inexpensive ways to honor her relationships, which allows her to meet her responsibilities to others as well as herself. Compared to Polly's offerings, Frieda's gifts reveal how much she values her friends, because Frieda spends considerable time and energy on providing something heartfelt, personal, and above all, of value to the recipient. She cares about what would please the important people in her life. Polly instead is focused only on saving money and cares little, if at all, about whether the recipients of her presents would want or need them.

Spending money you don't have, or being unwilling to spend money you do have, implicates all five principles of ethical intelligence. Keeping them in mind during the holidays — and throughout the year — will help you honor your financial obligations to yourself and your family, as well as maintain good, healthy relationships with the people you care about.

I NEVER TAKE VACATIONS!
A DUBIOUS DISTINCTION

In the seven years I've known her, I can't recall ever seeing my friend Maria take a vacation. Maria is blessed with doing a job she loves, so much so that she does it all the time, day in and day out. She works for herself and in her own home, so she is literally always on the job. But surely she's had *some* time off, right? Perhaps before we became friends almost a decade ago? So the other day I asked her how long it has been since she has had a vacation.

"Twenty years," she replied, without an ounce of sadness about this stunning fact. "I'm fortunate in being able to do what I love, and as the saying goes, if you love what you do, you'll never work a day in your life."

"Besides," she added, "if I don't work, I don't bring in any money, and that can't happen. And I'm single, so the idea of going on a trip by myself doesn't appeal to me at all. But the bottom line is that my work gives me a sense of purpose in life."

Maria wore her twenty vacationless years almost as a badge of honor. You probably know someone like Maria. Maybe *you* are someone like Maria. I'll explain why going so long without a vacation isn't something to be proud of but is instead a practice at odds with ethical intelligence.

An International Perspective

We have a lot of things to be proud of in the United States — freedom of the press, spectacular national parks, the films of John Ford — but mandatory paid vacation isn't one of them. Yet even small countries with struggling economies make sure that working people spend some time away from their jobs. Australians, Italians,

Latvians, and the Japanese get twenty days off each year; Swedes and Greeks get twenty-five; Lithuanians get twenty-eight; and the Finns and French get thirty.[6] Imagine taking up to six weeks of paid vacation each year and not feeling the slightest bit of guilt in doing so. It's not a fantasy; for many, it is a happy way of life.

Why doesn't the United States have vacation policies like Finland or Greece? Isn't time off really a perk or benefit akin to a year-end bonus? Employers aren't required to give employees extra money at Christmas; those that do are going above and beyond the call of duty. But why are we even discussing windsurfing in Hawaii or skiing in Aspen in the context of ethics?

Taking a vacation is an ethical issue for several reasons: you have an ethical responsibility to do your job to the best of your ability, and taking time off occasionally is a necessary condition for this; and the fifth principle of ethical intelligence, Be Loving, applies to how you treat yourself, not just others, and going for months or years without a vacation isn't a very kind way to treat yourself.

Employers may not have a legal responsibility to give employees time off from work, but the ethically intelligent ones do so anyway because they realize that a well-rested workforce is a productive one. Ethically intelligent people give themselves a break from time to time because they know that not only does this enable them to do their jobs well, but it's a marvelous thing in and of itself. "If it feels good, do it!" doesn't apply to everything, but it's the perfect salve for work-related burnout.

Common Excuses for Skipping Vacations

Let's now consider some of the most common reasons for not taking time off and how you can overcome them.

1. *I work for myself. / My employer doesn't provide paid vacations. / I've been laid off, and I need to work.* The reluctance to give up some future revenue is understandable, particularly in our current

economy. But how often is this an excuse rather than an accurate reflection of one's financial or work situation? Taking a vacation doesn't have to mean gambling big in Vegas or flying first-class to Sydney, as fun as these trips may be. With "staycations" becoming more popular, time away from work can mean nothing more than sleeping late, watching DVDs, and eating lots of comfort food at home. We budget for meals, clothing, and transportation. Shouldn't we also budget for a vacation? Yes, there ought to be a law mandating paid vacations, but until that comes to pass, we'll have to find creative ways on our own to take time off.

2. *I love my work, and I'm miserable when I'm away from it.* "I love my cigar, but I take it out of my mouth once in a while." This remark, attributed to Groucho Marx (perhaps falsely),[7] says it all: it's wonderful to be jazzed about one's job — I feel the same way — but a rich, meaningful life involves things beyond work.

3. *Most of the people I work with aren't taking vacations, so I don't want to burden them with the extra work they'd have if I left for a while.* It's praiseworthy to want to avoid causing undue stress on your colleagues, but you — and they — are entitled (ethically, if not legally) to some time off. Ultimately, the fair distribution of labor is a management issue, and employees shouldn't have to worry that a justifiable absence will result in an undue burden on the team.

4. *I'm the only one at work who can do my job — the company and my clients can't afford for me to be away.* It's nice to feel wanted or needed, but few of us are truly indispensable, as much as we may hate to admit it. I submit that in most cases, the idea that you, and only you, can do your job is a delusion of grandeur rather than a reflection of reality.

5. *I feel guilty when I take vacations.* If you're not yet convinced that it's ethically intelligent to take time off, perhaps it's time to talk with a trusted adviser about why you feel you aren't worthy of a

trip to the mountains or the shore, or even just some time to yourself. You have every reason to feel good about treating yourself right, and vacations, however you choose to spend them, are self-indulgent in the best possible way.

6. *I'm single and don't like the idea of going somewhere by myself.* As a survivor of the dating wars, I understand this feeling all too well. But a lot of people find someone to love while they're on vacation, and the relationship sometimes lasts far beyond the length of the trip itself. There are hiking trips, walking tours, and lots of other vacations one can take as a single person; finding out about these possibilities is just a Google search away.

7. *I can't leave work behind, so the best I can do is a working vacation.* The batteries you recharge on vacation shouldn't be the ones in your BlackBerry or iPhone. Checking email, taking work-related phone calls, and reading material related to one's job simply doesn't allow you to unwind completely, which is the whole point of your vacation in the first place. Doing your job while you sit in a chair on the beach is the worst of both worlds because you're not fully present in either one. Thus the concept of the working vacation makes about as much sense as showing up for a corporate job in shorts and a tank top with a margarita in your hand.

To the list of things for which there is a time — a time to be born, a time to die, a time to weep, a time to laugh — one might add a time to work and a time to take a long break.

LAYABOUTS, SCAM ARTISTS, AND AUDITORIUM HOPPERS: MAINTAINING GOOD RELATIONSHIPS WITH LOCAL BUSINESSES

What do the mall's megabookstore, a small, expensive dress shop, and your local multiplex cinema have in common? All create opportunities for customers to choose to treat the business in question with ethical intelligence or to take advantage of that business. After presenting stories in these three settings, I'll explain how the main character in each story has made, or has been tempted to make, an ethically unintelligent choice and what a better approach would be.

The Bookstore Bum

Harry loves to read, and he uses his library card regularly. The problem is that it takes his local library a long time to get the latest books, and their selection of magazines is spotty. Harry makes up for it by going to Bunch o' Books, the megabookstore at a nearby mall, which not only has a wide-ranging stock of books and magazines but also comfortable chairs, a quiet atmosphere, and a staff that doesn't seem to mind customers reading in the store for hours. Harry rarely buys anything since he can finish magazines and sometimes even books in a single visit. Sometimes he'll even bring lunch with him, and no one who works there ever tells him to stop.

One day, Martha, a neighbor of Harry's, spies Harry leafing through a copy of *Popular Science* while he munches on a cheese-and-tomato sandwich slathered with mayonnaise and brown mustard.

MARTHA. Hey there, Harry! Not a bad arrangement you got there, eh?

HARRY, *looking up with annoyance.* What's that supposed to mean? The store doesn't mind what I'm doing. What do you think these chairs are for, anyway?

MARTHA, *noticing that Harry's hands and the pages of the magazine are stained with grease.* So you're going to buy that magazine, now that you've messed it all up?

HARRY, *wondering why Martha is getting on his case.* It's not a big deal. You know, the store can return it to the publisher without losing a dime. Same with books.

MARTHA, *shaking her head disapprovingly.* Yeah, right.

HARRY, *feeling his blood pressure starting to rise.* Who are you, Paul Blart, mall cop?[8] Get lost!

MARTHA, *muttering under her breath as she walks away.* What a jerk!

Harry returns to his sandwich and magazine and picks up where he left off before Martha interrupted his pleasant afternoon.

The Free Dress

Esmeralda is beside herself: George, the guy she has been seeing for a short while, has invited her to go to La Louisianne, one of the fanciest restaurants in town. The problem is that Esmeralda can't afford to buy a new dress, and she doesn't want to wear any of the ones she has. So she calls her friend Joyce to ask for advice.

JOYCE. I'd lend you one of my outfits, but ———.

ESMERALDA. I know. We're not the same size.

JOYCE. I could have one altered for you.

ESMERALDA. Oh, you're so nice, Joyce, but I couldn't let you do that. I don't know what to do. I want to look good for George, but I don't have the money right now.

JOYCE. Just be honest with George. Tell him the truth: you're a single mom, and you're between jobs. If he's the right guy for you, he'll understand.

ESMERALDA. I don't want him to think I'm pressuring him to get me a dress. I'd just feel embarrassed wearing what I have to La Louisianne.

JOYCE. Well, there is one thing you could do.

ESMERALDA. What's that?

JOYCE. You're supposed to go out Friday night, right?

ESMERALDA. Yep.

JOYCE. Do you have some room on your credit card?

ESMERALDA. Uh, a little bit, yeah.

JOYCE. So get the dress you want at Rizzo's on Friday afternoon, wear it that night, and return it on Saturday. Rizzo's gives you fourteen days to return something, no questions asked.

ESMERALDA. For store credit?

JOYCE. Nope. A refund. Do it, Es! It's not a big deal.

Esmeralda hangs up the phone and feels troubled. She wants to look nice for George on Friday night, but something doesn't feel right about Joyce's plan. She decides to sleep on it and worry about it later.

Auditorium Hopping at the Multiplex

Alex and his friend Stu drive over to the Rialto, a twenty-five-screen cinema, to see the new Roger Rebar movie, *Heavy Duty MetalMan*. Two and a half hours later, they emerge from auditorium 12 and head for the exit.

STU, *as they walk by auditorium 10*. Hey, Alex, check it out! *Earth Invaders*, the new Joey Mandelbaum movie, starts in ten minutes!

ALEX. Nah. At these prices, one movie is all I can afford.

STU. Whaddaya mean? We can just walk right in. *(Stu is right. The only usher in the place is way down the hall, and he's busy vacuuming the carpet.)*

ALEX. What if we get caught?

STU. We won't. No one's around.

ALEX, *worried that something bad will happen*. I dunno.

STU. We're not hurting anyone. We already gave money to the theater. And the movie has been out for weeks. I'm sure there are plenty of seats available, and if we don't take them, they'll just be empty. *(Alex considers what Stu is saying.)* Besides, Alex, it's not cheating if you don't get caught! C'mon, man, the movie's gonna start soon!

Alex is torn: Stu is persuasive, but something still doesn't feel right.

If You *Can* Do It, You *Should* Do It, Right?

Harry has made an ethically unintelligent choice, and Esmeralda and Alex are tempted to do so. What could each do differently, and why is it important? It's time for answers.

No One's Wild about Harry

Bunch o' Books either allows the public to make use of its products and furniture without making a purchase, or it has no policy expressly forbidding the public from doing this, or its policy against loitering isn't being enforced. But whatever its policy happens to be, Harry is exploiting it for his own gain. The essence of the fourth principle of ethical intelligence, Be Fair, is that we ought to give others their due. A commercial bookstore isn't a charitable organization or a public library; its very existence depends upon people purchasing at least some of the items they peruse. This doesn't mean that everyone who enters its premises must buy a book, magazine, calendar, or birthday card. No one can rightly fault someone for taking a look at a few books and then walking out empty handed. But Harry is treating the merchandise as if he already owns it.

Another way that the principle of fairness is implicated in this scenario is that the books and magazines Harry is reading for free at Bunch o' Books didn't materialize from thin air; publishers, authors, distributors, and bookstore employees have invested their time and energy in bringing this material to the public. They're entitled to be compensated for their labor.

The fact that Harry brings his own food into the establishment may very well violate health department regulations, but even if it doesn't, this practice makes it easy for him to muck up the merchandise. Who would want to buy the *Popular Science* issue after Harry has gotten his greasy fingerprints all over it? Pawing a magazine one doesn't intend to buy while shoveling food in one's gullet isn't respectful of someone else's property and thus violates the third principle of ethical intelligence, Respect Others.

Harry is right about one thing: the store may indeed return its stock without penalty, but this arrangement among publishers, distributors, and booksellers exists in spite of, not because of, freeloaders like Harry. Harry's behavior doesn't trouble him, but it should because it violates the compact between businesses and customers that calls for each to give the other their due. Customers rightfully expect businesses to allow them to examine the merchandise before buying it. They also expect businesses not to sell them defective or damaged goods. By the same token, businesses have a right to expect customers not to take advantage of the right-to-examine policy and to avoid damaging their merchandise. Harry has treated Bunch o' Books unfairly, and his behavior is inconsistent with ethical intelligence.

Ethically intelligent bookstore patrons treat the merchandise — and by extension, the people who have produced it, distributed it, and may want to buy it — with respect. They also avoid treating bookstores, those quickly vanishing treasures of the community, like public libraries.

POSTSCRIPT. Harry doesn't live in my town, but there are enough people like him to have forced my local bookstore to close. The store was always filled with people, but it didn't make enough money to stay afloat. Not only did would-be patrons spend hour after hour reading books and magazines without buying them, but they also made notes about the books they did want to buy — then went home and ordered them online for less money. In the short run, these folks got some bargains, but their save-money-at-all-costs philosophy eventually cost them the very thing that made their cost-cutting measure possible in the first place: a well-stocked bookstore, which was no longer able to meet the needs of legitimate customers.[9]

A discount clothing store took its place, which provides a nice segue for considering whether Joyce's plan for Esmeralda to get a dress at no cost is an ethically intelligent thing to do.

The Clothing Store as Charity?

Rizzo's policy that allows patrons to return merchandise within fourteen days is based on good faith: Rizzo's trusts its customers to have a good reason for bringing a dress back (for example, it turned out to be uncomfortable after wearing it for a while). The policy obviously can't mean that a customer who buys a dress with the intention of wearing it only once is entitled to a full refund. How long could a business survive if it did that? A clothing store isn't a charity, and its very existence depends upon customers buying products — and keeping them. In other words, it is in a customer's own interest not to take unfair advantage of a store's return policy. If enough people like Esmeralda exploit the policy, the store might decide not to allow any returns — or it could even go out of business.

Imagine how Esmeralda would react if the store manager refused to let her have the dress because she is Latina, or she is a few pounds overweight, or he doesn't find her attractive. Esmeralda would justifiably be outraged because race, weight, or looks aren't legitimate bases for denying someone an opportunity to purchase something. A business that treats customers this way is not giving them their due and thus violates the fourth principle of ethical intelligence, Be Fair. (As an assault on a person's dignity, it also violates the Do No Harm principle, and it hardly upholds the Respect Others principle, either.) We expect businesses to be fair to customers, and by the same token, it's right to expect customers to be fair to businesses. Why should ethical responsibilities flow in only one direction in a relationship?

It's worth taking a step back and asking why Esmeralda feels it necessary to be someone she isn't (someone with a lot of money) in the first place. Treating her fancy date as a masquerade will only buy Esmeralda some time. Eventually, the truth will come out, and how impressed will George be after he learns that he has been duped? Joyce may not have the keenest ethical intelligence when it comes to treating businesses fairly, but she's right about one thing: Esmeralda should not feel ashamed about the sacrifices she has had to make as a single mom; these sacrifices show her to be a person of good character. I know how difficult it is when you want people to like you and are afraid that they won't if they know the truth about you. But Esmeralda is more likely to get what she wants — a good man to love her — if she honors the third principle of ethical intelligence, Respect Others, by not deceiving George and being up-front about her situation. Then she won't have to compromise the fourth principle of ethical intelligence, Be Fair, by taking unfair advantage of the clothing store's liberal return policy.

POSTSCRIPT. Esmeralda ignored the voice in her that said, "Don't do this; it's not right." She bought a beautiful dress for $750 with her credit card on Friday afternoon, wore it to La Louisianne Friday night, and returned it on Saturday. Joyce was right; Rizzo's did take the dress back, no questions asked. But what Joyce didn't know was that Rizzo's charges a 15 percent restocking fee for all returned items that aren't defective. Since there was nothing wrong with the dress, Esmeralda had to pay $112.50 for what can only be called a scam. The principle of fairness was ultimately upheld — in spite of Esmeralda's approach to business ethics, not because of it.

Everyone, including Esmeralda, will be better off next time if she makes choices consistent with the principles of ethical intelligence.

The Two-for-One Movie Deal

Stu believes there's nothing wrong with auditorium hopping at the multiplex, on the grounds that nobody is hurt by this practice. It's true that if he and Alex decide not to sneak into *Earth Invaders*, a screening that isn't sold out, the two seats they would have taken would go unused. But filling those seats without paying for the privilege does cause harm. It harms not just Joey Mandelbaum, the star of the movie, but everyone who worked on it. They toiled long and hard to make something that entertains people. As was the case with Harry, Alex and Stu would be enjoying the fruits of someone else's labor without paying for it, so everyone whose sweat equity went into producing, distributing, and exhibiting the film would be deprived of compensation they rightfully deserve. We see here how the principles Do No Harm and Be Fair can sometimes overlap; depriving someone of something he or she deserves harms that person.

It's also not fair to the people who paid good money to be there, and they too worked hard to be able to afford an afternoon at the movies (not an inexpensive proposition these days). Why should Alex and Stu be exempt from shelling out cash, too? By getting something for nothing, they'd essentially be stealing from the filmmakers and suggesting that they're somehow better than the folks who bought tickets to that show.

Alex and Stu presumably wouldn't think of walking into a drugstore and sticking a couple of candy bars into their pockets without paying for them, but the practice of auditorium hopping is, in effect, no different.

If Alex and Stu want to see the movie, the fair thing — the ethically intelligent thing — to do would be to go back to the box office, buy their tickets just like everybody else, and settle into two seats that they can now legitimately claim they have every right to sit in.

POSTSCRIPT. Alex and Stu decided to sneak into the theater after all. They watched the movie for free and left without being noticed.

Yes, it's possible to do something that's ethically unintelligent and get away with it. But it's still wrong.

SUMMARY

Making ethically intelligent choices with family, friends, and in your community includes the following.

- *Maintaining an ethically intelligent work-life balance by spending meaningful time at home and with friends.* There are periods when the balance has to tip in favor of work, but when the scale is permanently skewed toward your career, your valued relationships and your own well-being will be compromised.

- *Being frugal, but not in ways that compromise your connections with family and friends.* An ethically intelligent approach to money means not spending it when you don't have it and being appropriately generous when you do.

- *Taking periodic vacations.* Recharging your batteries enables you to better serve your clients when you return to work, and vacations with family or friends give you meaningful time alone with them.

- *Treating local businesses respectfully and fairly.* This means recognizing that bookstores aren't libraries, clothing stores aren't charities, and a ticket to one movie at the multiplex isn't a free pass to all the other films showing there.

CHAPTER 10

If I Am Not for Myself, Who Will Be?
Ethical Intelligence with Yourself

Hillel, a twelfth-century Jewish leader and scholar, said, "If I am not for myself, who will be? But if I am for myself only, what am I?" This quotation crystallizes the central challenge for living an ethically intelligent life: honoring your responsibilities to yourself as well as to others. Too often, it seems, we tilt in one direction or the other. Up to now, we've looked at ethically intelligent ways of dealing with other people. It's now time to reflect on the other half of the equation: you. We'll do so with respect to five issues:

- Multitasking
- Use of technology
- Healthy living
- Anger
- Being downsized

MULTITASKING MADNESS

Vanessa met me outside my hotel, cell phone in hand. "I'm sorry," she mouthed and continued with what appeared to be an important call. Vanessa was a member of a group that had hired me to give an after-dinner speech, and she had volunteered to pick me up and escort me to the venue.

I stood around for a few minutes, going over the speech in my head, and was anxious to get going. But Vanessa was quite absorbed in her conversation. She signaled me to get into her car, conveniently parked in front of the hotel. I figured she was about to wrap things up. But she continued as we sat in her motionless car. When she pulled a key ring out of her purse, I figured we would finally be heading to the venue. And I was right — but the call continued as she started the car and pulled out of the parking space.

"I don't mind if we wait here a little while," I said, trying not to seem too confrontational about her decision to drive while using her cell phone.

"It's okay," she replied, without any apparent awareness of the dangers of what she was doing.

"This is one of the issues I'll be speaking about tonight, actually," I proclaimed with a greater sense of urgency. "The ethics of multitasking behind the wheel."

She laughed.

"I'm serious. I'd rather you just pull over and continue your conversation while we're parked."

She waved me off as if I were asking her to do something burdensome.

Since I was sitting in the organ-donor seat, I had to do something drastic. "Vanessa, please let me out. I'm happy to take a cab." We pulled over, and she did her best to end the call; but it went on for another ten minutes.

When the yak fest finally ended, she explained that she had to deal with a crisis at work. I told her that I appreciated the situation she was in but that driving with a cell phone in her hand was putting people — including us — at risk. I'm not sure I got through to her, but there was a happy ending of sorts: I was able to deliver my speech in person rather than via webcam from the emergency room.

Vanessa wasn't a bad person, but she wasn't a good manager, either. A multitasker behind a desk is unproductive. A multitasker behind the wheel of a car is a potential killer.

The term *multitasking* suggests that it's possible to do several worthwhile things at the same time, but emerging evidence suggests that this is a fantasy because our brains are built to monotask. When we multitask, we're doing a lot of work, but we're not doing most (or any) of it well.[1] Psychiatrist Edward M. Hallowell, author of *CrazyBusy*, puts it this way: "Multitasking is shifting focus from one task to another in rapid succession. It gives the illusion that we're simultaneously tasking, but we're really not. It's like playing tennis with three balls."[2] (I can only imagine how Michael Scott from *The Office* would react to that last line.)

A study from the Virginia Tech Transportation Institute found that when truck drivers texted, their collision risk was twenty-three times as great as when not texting, and University of Utah researchers showed that talking on a cell phone while driving quadruples the rate of crashing, a statistic equal to what happens when people drive drunk.[3] As of this writing, twenty-five states have outlawed texting behind the wheel for all drivers, and seven others have made the practice illegal for underage drivers or those with learner's permits.[4] Of course, even in states where there is no law against texting while driving, it's still ethically unintelligent to engage in this practice. Recall from the discussion in chapter 4 that the principles of ethical intelligence apply even without the force of law behind them.

Let's now examine our obsession with technology and consider some ethically intelligent ways to deal with the gadgets that seem to have overtaken our lives.

SMART PHONES AND STUPID CHOICES

Technology is neither ethically intelligent nor blatantly unethical. It can't be either of those things because it has no will of its own.

It's just a thing, an instrument. We can put it to good use if we so choose, we can waste our time with it, or we can hurt people with it. The choice is ours. And we're choosing to use it in all of these ways, every single day.

Facebook, for example, allows us to get back in touch with friends from high school we haven't heard from in years. A fifth-grade classmate of mine got ahold of me through Facebook and let me know that our beloved teacher was alive and well, even though I'd been told by the school where he worked that he'd died decades ago! I'd never have gotten this great news had it not been for Facebook.

But Facebook can provide an unwelcome distraction when you're trying to get work done on the computer. It's just so easy to click on that tab to post something, send a message to a friend, or look at everyone's updates. That's not Facebook's fault, but its ease of access makes it so tempting to shift our focus from the valuable or necessary to the trivial. Attorney Forest Jackson Bowman makes a distinction between tasks that are urgent and those that are important;[5] the ready access that texts, email, phone calls, and the Internet afford makes it easy to confuse these two categories. We may feel a sense of urgency to log on to Facebook, but how important is it to do so?

A bank executive I know frequently complains about how distracted her boss is during staff meetings. The boss — I'll call him Eric — reads and writes email and makes calls while briefing the staff. "I'll ask Eric a question about an assignment he's given us," my friend complains, "but he's so immersed in what he's doing that I have to repeat my question a couple of times. It ends up taking me three times as long to communicate with him."

Since multitasking interferes with the ability to do one's job well, the good manager sets an example by focusing on one task at a time. You can't expect the people you lead to resist the urge to multitask if you can't do so yourself. You've probably been annoyed when a clerk is more interested in his or her phone conversation than in assisting you. Why, then, is it okay to do the same thing when you're working with your team?

In Control or Being Controlled?

I'm not sure whether BlackBerrys and iPhones cause attention problems or simply make those who are susceptible more prone to them. Yes, I know it's hard to put those devices away, even for a few moments. It doesn't help that everywhere we go, we're surrounded by people who are absorbed in their electronic gadgets.[6] What it comes down to is this: Are you controlling the technology, or is the technology controlling you?

An actor I once knew had a catchy slogan on his business card: "Always there. Always *on*!" It was a memorable way to let casting directors know of his commitment to his work.

Your boss may expect you to be always available to him or her, whether or not you're technically on the job. But this isn't fair. You deserve to have time away from work, and your company should respect your downtime. If you're concerned that your boss would balk at such an idea, you might want to explain that having some downtime makes sense from a business perspective. Having the freedom to recharge your batteries and putting aside the pressure to be "always there, always on" means you are more likely to do good work when you're on the job.

The same goes for others who want or expect you to be always available. It's one thing to be on call for an ill family member, but must you have your cell phone on at all times just so you don't miss a call?

Using technology in an ethically intelligent way calls for the following.

1. *Do one thing at a time.* Focusing on the task at hand is the best way to get the job done. Multitasking may feel effective, but it isn't.

Monotasking maximizes your own productivity and serves as a positive example to others. A fabulous software application called Freedom allows you to disconnect from the Internet for however much time you wish. Writers such as Nora Ephron, Nick Hornby, Dave Eggers, and Seth Godin use it regularly; if you lack the discipline to unplug yourself, you should, too.[7]

2. *Respect the personal lives of others.* It may take only a few seconds to write and send an email or a text, but it's wrong to expect recipients to respond just as quickly. Boundaries are good, and ethically intelligent people honor them.

3. *Don't allow others to multitask while driving.* When you're on the phone with a friend, family member, or coworker who tells you that he or she is behind the wheel, say, "Please hang up and call me back when you're out of harm's way, or I'll call you back shortly."

4. *Give yourself a break.* You're entitled to watch a movie all the way through or to have a nice meal without looking at your email. And let's face it: there aren't many emails so urgent they can't wait a few hours.

5. *Remember why they're called "sick days" and "vacation."* If you're too sick to come to the office, you're entitled to convalesce without feeling pressured to work at home. If you're on vacation, you deserve to enjoy time on the beach without checking your email and voice mail. You may have lost a family member or be with one who has just gotten married: if ever there was a time when you ought to be free from multitasking, surely it's this.

There is a larger problem than multitasking when it comes to our obsession with technology. I call it "iSolation."

iSolation Insanity

In 1997, Apple began using the phrase "Think different" in its advertising campaign, and the phrase quickly became as iconic as "Where's the beef?" and "Got milk?" On June 29, 2007, the company released the iPhone, and the world has never been the same. This combination of cell phone, iPod, camera, and web browser was the sleekest, hippest consumer-electronic device we'd seen in years, and the only invention that has gotten more press is Apple's own iPad. What could be wrong with owning high-tech toys that promise to make our lives easier and more fun?

A lot, as it turns out.

Our society has devolved into a mass of turned-on, tuned-out, and plugged-in technophiles. Whatever distinction used to exist between public and private life is all but gone, as one can witness on any city street, bus, or plane, or in any shopping mall. Waiting in line at the grocery store or post office used to mean striking up a conversation with the person in front of you. It now involves blurting the intimate details of one's love life into a cell phone for all to hear, or scrolling through a playlist for just the right song, or surfing the web for something we want but don't really need.

There are three major costs associated with this iSolation.

The first is an opportunity cost. Our social fabric is in danger of being ripped to shreds as we swap personal relationships for electronic connection. The very nature of community depends upon us being connected to one another as human beings, not merely as digital representations. Being civil means, or at least used to mean, valuing our relationships beyond our immediate circle of family and friends. If upon leaving home, we immerse ourselves in idle chatter on the phone, listen to music nonstop at volume levels that preclude hearing the world around us, read every piece of email sent since the last time we checked, or hunt for bargains on the Internet, we miss the chance on the way to work to make new friendships, renew old ones, say hello to a stranger, or simply notice the world around us. A community is not merely a collection of individuals. It is a web (in the traditional sense of the word) of interconnectedness, and this web cannot exist for long if each of its constituents is concerned primarily or exclusively with himself or herself. It is hard to apply any of the principles of ethical intelligence when we separate ourselves from the world around us.

The second cost of iSolation is to our psychological health. I don't know about you, but my best ideas come when I'm either doing something mundane like brushing my teeth or simply daydreaming. That's right, daydreaming. A waste of time, you say? Not at all. To be creative is to have the freedom to dream, to let thoughts appear and evaporate, and — yes — to play. "But I'm too busy to play," you reply. Nonsense. Some of the time spent fidgeting with a cell phone or MP3 player is time we could put to better use, such as by doing nothing at all. When our brains are constantly stimulated by electronic data, they are, of necessity, precluded from taking anything else in, such as the random thoughts that can be the genesis of great ideas. The nonstop avalanche of images and sounds from electronic media (among other distractions) is a barrier, not a portal, to creativity. Our technological obsession threatens a crucial component of ethical intelligence: treating ourselves with care.

The third cost of our absorption in technology is the most serious of all: the possibility of an increased risk of injury and mortality. In the previous section, I referred to several studies that have quantified these risks for people who talk or text while driving. You may dispute this research, but imagine that your son or daughter has just gotten a driver's license and is taking your car out for a spin. Would it matter to you if other drivers are yakking away on a cell phone while cruising next to, or heading toward, your child? Of course it would, and it should. Driving is challenging enough without having to worry about people around you being literally driven to distraction. We are, to borrow a phrase from the late author Neil Postman, "amusing ourselves to death."[8] Remember that saying "Friends don't let friends drive drunk"? To this we should now add, "or text, talk, and email from behind the wheel." The first principle of ethical intelligence, Do No Harm, demands nothing less.

It's not only drivers whose technological distractions pose a risk to themselves and others; pedestrians are to blame, too. New York State senator Carl Kruger reintroduced a bill that would ban people from using cell phones, MP3 players, and other electronic devices while crossing the street anywhere in the state, and Arkansas is considering similar legislation.[9] When you're out for a stroll, it is hard enough to be on guard against drivers who are immersed in their cell phone conversations, emails, or texts. It's harder still when you're absorbed in your own electronic gadget. Walking while texting poses risks even in a shopping mall, as a popular YouTube video demonstrates.[10]

None of what I am saying is a call to return to the days when people got their entertainment by huddling together in front of a radio (though that sounds pretty good, if you ask me). Nor is it an indictment of capitalism and the push to sell bigger, better, newer, and faster gizmos. There's nothing wrong with that, as far as it goes. After all, technology is morally neutral. It can be put to useful or harmful purposes.

So if the ever-increasing opportunities for technological distraction result in more self-absorption, less time to daydream, and more pedestrian and driver accidents, it won't be the fault of Apple, or the IT industry as a whole, or Madison Avenue, or the news media, or the automobile industry, or anyone else we care to blame. It will be our own fault. But it's not too late to think different.

DEEP-FRIED BUTTERBALLS WITH EXTRA GRAVY: THE ETHICS OF HEALTHY LIVING

An out-of-order elevator sent Stieg Larsson climbing seven flights of stairs to his office. When he reached the top, he died of a massive heart attack — at the age of fifty.[11] Larsson, the author of *The Girl with the Dragon Tattoo* and its two sequels, is one of the most successful writers of adult fiction today, but he never got to experience his worldwide celebrity while he was alive. Why not? There is good reason to believe that his lack of exercise, excessive smoking, and steady diet of junk food were major factors in Larsson's death. His refusal to take his health as seriously as he took his work wasn't unfortunate. It was ethically unintelligent, even tragic. His legions of fans are now deprived of experiencing more of his formidable literary talent, and Larsson himself is deprived of enjoying the fruits of his achievements and his very life.

Health isn't usually presented as an ethical issue, but it may very well be the most important ethical issue of all. After all, without your health, you aren't able to do many of the things that make life worth living. It's true that there is a genetic component to health, so it's not fair to attribute all forms of poor health to personal choice. There is also a socioeconomic element; poor neighborhoods often lack ready access to fresh fruits and vegetables, which creates significant obstacles to maintaining a healthy diet.

Nevertheless, too many of us are unwell not because of our DNA or socioeconomic status but because we don't place a high enough value on our health. It should be liberating, not burdensome, to realize that we can control our destinies by making smart choices about diet, exercise, and other elements of good health. I'll explain how the five principles of ethical intelligence exhort us to make such choices, and I'll suggest some specific ways for doing so.

Body, Mind, and Spirit:
Applying the Principles of Ethical Intelligence to Yourself

Mind

If someone rubs you the wrong way, the first principle of ethical intelligence, Do No Harm, means resisting the impulse to call that person an idiot or a moron, as much as you'd like to (and as apt as the label might be). Yet you may have no problem regarding yourself harshly if you don't live up to your own high standards in some way. But if it's ethically unintelligent to curse at others, it's also ethically unintelligent to curse at yourself.

Body

Assume you've invited some friends over for dinner to your house. Would you root around in the dumpster for some garbage to serve them? Of course not. But some of the food and drink you may choose to consume isn't much better than this. David Zinczenko and Matt Goulding's *Eat This, Not That!* has a picture of a popular restaurant's breakfast that includes a deep-fried steak smothered in gravy, three flapjacks, three eggs, and a side of hash browns.[12] This gut-busting, coronary artery–clogging monstrosity has 2,400 calories, 55 grams of saturated fat, 159 grams of carbohydrates, and 4,500 milligrams of sodium and is more than enough food for three people. But every day in America, thousands of people wolf this nutritional nightmare down, apparently without much concern for the bodily damage it causes. Even if you argue that corporate America has a right to produce such meals, it doesn't follow that it's right for you to indulge in them. If you take the Do No Harm principle at all seriously, as ethically intelligent people do, and if you're not training for a marathon or the Olympics, it's hard to justify eating such a breakfast at any time, for any reason.

You also violate this principle if you don't exercise regularly.

According to Adrian Bauman of the University of Sydney in Australia: "Physical inactivity is a major risk factor for death and for illness. It contributes to about one-sixth of heart disease...about the same for diabetes, about 12 percent for falls in the elderly, and about a tenth of all breast cancer and colon cancer are attributable to being physically inactive."[13]

But it's more ethically intelligent to give positive reasons *for* doing something than negative reasons for *not* doing it. Thus it's better to consider how exercise fulfills the second principle of ethical intelligence, Make Things Better, than how not exercising violates the first principle. On its website, the Mayo Clinic states that regular exercise:

- Improves your mood
- Combats chronic diseases
- Helps you manage your weight
- Boosts your energy level
- Promotes better sleep
- Enhances your sex life[14]

Even if you take issue with their claim that exercise is fun, the above benefits represent some of the best ways to make things better for yourself.

Spirit

Finally, let's not forget that you have not just a body and a mind but a spirit as well. Medical science is just beginning to recognize what yoga instructors, Tibetan monks, and rock stars have known for years: meditation is one of the best ways to renew, refresh, and revitalize. You can do it almost anywhere, it costs nothing, and the benefits are both physiological and psychological: lowered blood pressure, a sense of calm that lasts far beyond the period of meditation itself, and the ability to focus on doing one thing at a time (which alone makes the practice worth pursuing). Even if you recognize the importance of exercising, eating well, and avoiding smoking, it can be difficult to realize these goals. Meditation makes it much easier to do so. In the appendix, I discuss some of the material I've found helpful for developing and maintaining a meditation practice.

I'M MAD AS H-E-DOUBLE HOCKEY STICKS! ETHICALLY INTELLIGENT ANGER

All we have to do is open the newspaper, turn on the TV, or look at the world around us, and it won't take long to find something that makes us mad. Whether it's the high price of groceries and gas, the indignities of air travel, or the person in the next cubicle yakking loudly on a cell phone during working hours, we encounter plenty of things every day that keep our blood pressure at an unhealthy high.

It can be harmful to others and ourselves to vent our anger, but it can also be unhealthy and unwise to keep it bottled up. I will therefore offer five guidelines that make anger work for us instead of against us and that are grounded in the principles of ethics. I'll also show how these guidelines can be applied to three common and frustrating situations at work: the annoying coworker, the incompetent assistant, and the hands-off boss. But first, let's take a look at what anger is, and why this emotion raises ethical issues.

Is Anger Inevitable?

Anger is the intense feeling associated with a real or perceived injustice. When you're trying to enjoy a movie and the person next to you carries on a conversation with his companion in a normal tone of voice, you get angry because you feel he is doing something he shouldn't be doing. Employees who spend too much time at work making personal phone calls or surfing the Internet incur the wrath of their boss and their colleagues because they're doing something they shouldn't be doing (and not doing something they should be doing, namely, their work).

Although the experience of anger is psychological, its roots are in the realm of ethics; we get angry when we believe others have violated their ethical obligations to treat us with respect or to be fair — in other words, when people disregard the third and fourth principles of ethical intelligence as they apply to us.

Ethics plays a role not just in what gives rise to our anger but in what we choose to do with it. The expression of anger can be harmful, and we have an ethical obligation to do no harm. Domestic violence, sexual assault, and murder are the most extreme examples of what happens when anger gets out of hand.

But death and physical trauma are not the only harms that can result from the free expression of anger. Insulting, threatening, or demeaning a person can produce feelings of anxiety or fear that are forms of harm, even if that person emerges without bruises or broken bones. Taking ethics seriously and being a person of conscience therefore means, in part, ensuring our anger doesn't get out of hand.

Five Rules of Engagement

Thich Nhat Hanh, whom I mentioned in the section on giving criticism in chapter 6, notes that some people believe a good way to deal with anger is to beat up a pillow.[15] However, he finds this makes us feel worse because we intensify the very feelings we're trying to dissipate. Keeping our anger bottled up isn't an acceptable solution either, since doing so won't change the situation we're angry about and we're more likely to erupt with hostility somewhere down the line, which benefits no one. What, then, are some better ways of dealing with anger?

Here are my suggestions for responding with ethical intelligence when you encounter a situation that makes you angry:

1. *Stop.* Don't react right away. Take some time to assess what is going on.
2. *Breathe deeply.* Cooling down will make it easier to come up with a strategy that will succeed.
3. *Look at the matter from another point of view.* What are all of the possible explanations for why this is happening?
4. *Ask,* "What response is most likely to be effective?" It probably won't involve blowing your stack.
5. *Get help if need be.* The problem may be too big to handle alone. Help can even be in the form of some feedback from another person.

This is a commonsense approach to tackling infuriating situations with a cool head. Decisions made when we're boiling with rage rarely turn out to be good ones. How might we apply this five-step approach in our daily lives?

The Annoying Coworker

Whether it's their music played too loudly, personal phone conversations that go on and on, or too frequent visits to your office that waste time, coworkers can really get on your nerves, can't they? It's tempting to tell them to shut up or get lost. But not only is this disrespectful; it's not likely to get you what you want.

Instead of quietly seething, only to erupt in anger when you can't take it anymore, why not let the annoying person know as kindly as possible that what he or she is doing is making it difficult for you to get your work done, and then state whatever it is you'd like to have happen? The only way for us to have our needs met is to make it clear to others what those needs are.

The Incompetent Assistant

When people who work for you can't meet your standards, berating them and saying demeaning things is, as in the situation above, disrespectful and ineffective. The problem could be that your assistant is intimidated by you, and fear is getting in the way of the person's doing a good job. It could also be that the talents and skills this person has aren't matched by the job assignment. It might even be the case that your standards are too high, and no one — not even you — could reasonably be expected to meet them.

Isn't it in your own interest to try to find out what is really going on? Falling into the familiar pattern of getting angry, not getting the results you want, and then getting angrier won't accomplish anything. As the saying goes, "If you do what you've always done, you'll get what you've always gotten."

The Hands-Off Boss

Some bosses get on your nerves because they're always on your case, but it's just as bad, if not worse, to have a supervisor who has too little involvement in your work. A good manager has to be present and can't assume subordinates will be able to figure out what he or she wants. It is understandable to feel anger at being given tasks to do and little or no direction for how to do them; a manager who isn't around often is someone who appears not to care.

This is where looking at the situation from a different perspective can help: rather than being uncaring, the absentee manager may simply be overcommitted or even unaware that others want or need direction. Your solution, then, is to get involved, not mad. Letting the boss know what bothers you and what you'd like to change will benefit everyone: the company, your clients, and yourself. You have a right to be treated respectfully and fairly by your boss and every-one else with whom you work.

Of course, the five-step method for dealing with anger doesn't apply to every possible situation. The bigger the issue — global warming, terrorism, our collapsing economy — the more complex the solution. Complicated problems also may not have an immedi-ately identifiable party with whom we can work things out. Nev-ertheless, many of the frustrating situations we encounter can be helped by the solutions I've presented here.

WHEN YOU'VE BEEN DOWNSIZED

Even before the global economic crisis occurred in late 2008, anxi-ety about employment was high; at the beginning of that year, the U.S. Department of Labor released a report stating that there had been a net loss of sixty-three thousand jobs, which was the biggest monthly decline in five years.[16]

Whether or not your own job is in jeopardy in the near future, at some point in your career, you may become a victim of down-sizing (if you haven't already). What would an ethically intelligent response be? What should you avoid doing at all costs? The five principles that have served us well so far will again be valuable here.

You might be wondering what being downsized has to do with ethics at all. Let's take a look.

Being laid off is one of the most traumatic events we can expe-rience. On the Holmes-Rahe stress scale, getting fired is the eighth most stressful life experience, behind the death of a spouse (which is number 1) or going to jail (number 4), but ahead of the death of a close friend (number 17), foreclosure on a mortgage or loan (number 21), or in-law troubles (number 24).[17] Rightly or wrongly, many of us define ourselves by our jobs, which is why one of the first questions we ask someone we meet is, "What do you do?"

In chapter 6, I showed why downsizing has ethical implications for the bearers of bad news. But ethical issues are also at stake for those on the receiving end. If you've ever been downsized, I'll bet your first response was, "That's not fair!" Even if your company had — or believes it had — good reasons to eliminate your position, from your point of view, it feels as though an injustice has occurred. So the fourth principle of ethical intelligence, Be Fair, is implicated.

But that's not the only principle at work. When you ask yourself, "How will I be able to pay my bills now?" the underlying question is, "How can I meet my responsibilities to my family, myself, and those to whom I owe money?" All of these responsibilities are ethical ones and are applications of the first three principles of ethical intelligence, Do No Harm, Make Things Better, and Respect Others.

Finally, we've all known people who let the loss of their job get the better of them, so the fifth principle of ethical intelligence, which calls upon us to treat everyone — including ourselves — with compassion, is involved too.

Six Rules for Being Downsized with Ethical Intelligence

I propose the following guidelines for you to consider, should you find yourself suddenly out of a job.

1. *Get angry — later.* It's easy to react with hostility when you're told that your position is being eliminated. Don't. The suggestions I made in the previous section for corralling your anger are especially relevant in this circumstance. It's only human to be terribly upset or even filled with rage, but acting on those feelings may violate the Do No Harm principle. You won't regret holding back, but you will regret losing your cool.

2. *Don't take it personally.* We'd like to be able to control our lives and shape our destiny through the sheer force of will, but sometimes things happen to us that have absolutely nothing to do with what we've done or who we are. This is one of those times.

3. *Get a recommendation.* One of the best ways for a potential employer to find out how valuable you are is to hear from your current boss, but you may have to be the one to make this happen. Get a recommendation in writing as soon as possible. Volunteer to write it yourself. If a letter is out of the question or doesn't arrive in a timely fashion, ask your boss to send you a short email; even a one- or two-line testimonial will do. Get your boss's permission to put his or her direct phone number on your résumé and give it out at job interviews. (Incidentally, failure to follow guideline 1 could make this an impossibility. Burning bridges in the heat of anger is the worst thing you can do to yourself.)

4. *Be a self-promoter.* We're raised to believe that it's wrong to toot our own horn, but if ever there was a time to put that belief aside, it's now. Recalling the Hillel quotation that heads this chapter, one of our greatest challenges is striking the right balance between self-absorption and devotion to others. Still, there is not only no harm in standing up for yourself; it is unethical not to do so. Believing in yourself is one of the best ways of applying the principle of compassion to your own life. Consider this as well: How can others benefit from your expertise if you don't get the word out?

5. *Allow yourself to grieve.* Grief is a natural and healthy response to losing something or someone of value in your life, and taking your grief seriously is another important way to treat yourself with kindness. It is a sign of strength, not weakness, to seek counseling in the wake of being downsized. If you sustained an injury to your back, you would have no qualms about getting physical therapy. Why shouldn't you seek the appropriate remedy when your world

is turned upside down? Many of us still attach a stigma to psychotherapy — wrongly so.

6. *Accentuate the positive.* Is it possible that one of the worst things that could happen to you might turn out to be the best? Take a look at Harvey Mackay's *We Got Fired!...And It's the Best Thing That Ever Happened to Us.*[18] Michael Bloomberg, Muhammad Ali, Billie Jean King, Home Depot founder Bernie Marcus, Lee Iacocca, and Robert Redford are just a few of the wildly successful people who explain how losing a job led to something much better. Yes, it's dispiriting to get laid off, but Mackay's book reminds us of the riches that may lie just beyond the horizon, which would have been unavailable had we stayed where we were.

Bottom line: Taking the high road is challenging enough when all is going well. The real test of your character is how you respond when things are at their worst. Following the guidelines above will help you show the world — and yourself — that nothing, not even the loss of your job, can hold you back from success.

SUMMARY

Treating yourself with the same dignity and respect with which you treat others is an ethically intelligent thing to do. It is not an indulgence, and it's not something to feel guilty about.

Multitasking/Use of Technology

If we're constantly plugged in, turned on, and tuned out, we miss out on being a part of a real, as opposed to a virtual, community. Being overly fond of our electronic gadgets can be deadly, if we choose to multitask behind the wheel. Ethically intelligent people recognize the allure of these gizmos but don't let them control their lives — or extinguish them.

Healthy Living

Your body isn't a garbage dump, and treating it that way with a steady diet of junk food isn't a compassionate way to regard yourself. Neither is criticizing yourself excessively or neglecting your spiritual life.

Anger

The challenge in evincing anger in an ethically intelligent way is to recognize the problem at hand without letting it get the better of you. As Elizabeth Kenny said, "He who angers you conquers you."[19]

Being Downsized

Being downsized presents a supreme test of your ethical intelligence. By allowing yourself to grieve, being prudent in how and when you express your anger, shoring up recommendations, and above all, having continued faith in your abilities, you can turn a tragedy into a professional and personal triumph.

Epilogue

"**S**o what?" Roger Sublett, president of the Union Institute & University and former director of the Kellogg National Fellowship Program, likes to ask the people who go through his rigorous programs this question. On the page, this question sounds off-putting, even hostile, but coming from Sublett, it is a pure expression of loving-kindness. He insists that his students and fellows be prepared to answer this question before embarking on the leadership and scholarly programs he administers, and at every step of the way toward their conclusion. Without knowing the purpose of the journey from A to B, why waste everyone's time, energy, money, and other valuable resources making the journey?

Now that we've explored many facets of ethical intelligence, it's high time for us to answer Sublett's question. The good news is that, unlike the quiz at the beginning of the book, there are lots of right answers to it. Here are some valid responses to anyone who, upon learning that you've read this book, asks you, "So what?"

- The five principles of ethical intelligence help you make the best decisions possible, because they bring out the best in you.

- Life is easier when you're honest, because you don't have to remember which lies you told, when you told them, or who you told them to.

- There are lots of ways to get people to buy what you're selling, but the only way to keep them coming back is by earning their trust. The best way to do this is by running your business with ethical intelligence, which means hiring men and women who share this commitment and treating them — and yourself — with respect, fairness, and love.

- Striving to live according to the principles of ethical intelligence — as difficult as this can be — is the best way to get the things you want from life.

Making ethically intelligent choices is both an honorable and a beneficial way to live. It respects the rights of others, and in the long run, everyone ends up better off — including you.

How do *you* answer the question "So what?" I'd like to know. Contact me through my website, TheEthicsGuy.com.

The Five Questions

No matter how complex the subject, one should be able capture its essence on a single page. So this is what ethical intelligence comes down to.

When considering a course of action, ask yourself:

1. Will this avoid causing harm?
2. Will it make things better?
3. Is it respectful?
4. Is it fair?
5. Is it a loving thing to do?

If you can answer yes to each of these questions, it's an ethically intelligent thing to do.

If you can't, what other course of action will allow you to do so?

The five principles of ethical intelligence are a framework, not a formula, for living honorably. Managing your business and the rest of your life is a constant struggle, but if you make the five principles the foundation of your life, you'll be able to solve the toughest problems everywhere you go.

Books, Movies, and TV Shows That Will Enrich Your Ethical Intelligence

BOOKS

If you'd like to continue your study of ethics and ethical intelligence, here are some books you may find useful. It's a highly idiosyncratic list and hardly an exhaustive survey; but all of the works are informative, and some are even entertaining.

Aristotle. *Nicomachean Ethics*. Translated by Martin Ostwald. Indianapolis: Bobbs-Merrill, 1962.

There are two platforms upon which ethics, and thus ethical intelligence, rests: conduct and character. That is, we can talk about what we ought to do, or we can talk about who we ought to be. The framework for the first is made up of principles; for the second, it is virtues. Following the Beauchamp-Childress model (see p. 194), I have used a principle-based approach in shaping the discussion and have not mentioned virtues at all. Yet a full appreciation of the ethically intelligent life must take virtues into account, and it is to Aristotle we must turn to do so.

Ethical virtue speaks to excellence of character. For example, it's one thing to say, "You ought to do something rather than nothing if your boss has a drinking problem," but quite another to be able to take action. The same is true for the CEO who becomes ill and has to take a leave of absence. It's not easy to accept the fact that no one will live forever, but it must be done anyway. In both situations, the virtue of courage is needed, and Aristotle devotes considerable attention to explaining what it is and how to develop it.

In a future volume of the *Ethical Intelligence* series, I will explore the role that virtues play in the ethically intelligent life. But before I do, you will find *Nicomachean Ethics* to be indispensable reading. There are many translations available; I mention Ostwald's only because it is the one I have studied.

Tom L. Beauchamp and James F. Childress. *Principles of Biomedical Ethics*. 6th ed. New York: Oxford University Press, 2008.

As I mention in the acknowledgments, *Ethical Intelligence* rests firmly on the shoulders of this monumental, highly influential work. The principle-based approach to ethics, along with the actual principles I've presented, are derived from Beauchamp and Childress's book. To avoid repetition, I'll leave it at that for now, but suffice it to say that *Principles of Biomedical Ethics* is nothing short of a masterpiece. If my approach to ethics resonates with you, then you owe it to yourself to read Beauchamp and Childress's book posthaste.

Deborah J. Bennett. *Logic Made Easy: How to Know When Language Deceives You*. New York: Norton, 2005.

The only problem with learning even a few fundamentals of logic is that you'll get depressed when you see how many examples of illogic there are out there. Politicians, pundits, journalists, professors and teachers, your friends and family, and perhaps from time to time, even you, commit at least some of the fallacies described in Bennett's book. This is far from a trivial matter because a person's fallacious arguments about x give us no basis to decide whether x is true. I cited one type of fallacy, ad hominem attacks, in the section on ethically unintelligent criticism, but it's useful to know about many of the other sorts of bogus reasoning you encounter on a daily basis. Although I am loath to admit it, the book you have just read may include a few fallacies (though I've done my level best to ensure it does not).

Other books about logic and critical thinking that I like are Madsen Prie, *How to Win Every Argument: The Use and Abuse of Logic* (London: Continuum Books, 2007); and Anthony Weston, *A Rulebook for Arguments*, 4th ed. (Indianapolis: Hackett, 2008).

Dale Carnegie. *How to Win Friends and Influence People*. Rev. ed. New York: Pocket Books, 1981.

In chapter 2, I discussed Carnegie's book with respect to the fifth principle of ethical intelligence, and for its simple but profound insights, it's well worth reading (or rereading, if it has been a while). It's not explicitly about ethics, but many of the suggestions in *How to Win Friends and Influence People* do in fact show how to apply the five principles of ethical intelligence in daily life.

In my efforts to teach ethical intelligence across the country, I've also benefited greatly from Carnegie's book *The Quick and Easy Way to Effective Speaking: Modern Techniques for Dynamic Communication* (New York: Pocket Books, 1990). *The Quick and Easy Way to Effective Speaking* is a revision by Dale's wife, Dorothy, of his book *Public Speaking and Influencing Men in Business*, first published in 1913.

Daniel Clowes. *Wilson*. Montreal: Drawn and Quarterly, 2010.

What in the world does a graphic novel about a self-absorbed do-nothing have to do with ethical intelligence? A lot, actually. This deeply moving story shows the dangers of focusing obsessively on our own needs and desires. Ethics, as I've suggested throughout this book, is about balancing duties to self and duties to others. It's useful to see what can happen when you take other people out of the picture. Wilson longs for connection but can't bring himself to do it (at least in a legal way). A heartbreaking — but also, in places, laugh-out-loud funny — work of art.

H. Tristram Engelhardt Jr. *The Foundations of Bioethics*. 2nd ed. New York: Oxford University Press, 1995.

This is, quite simply, one of the most brilliant and astonishing books I've ever read. You may not agree with many of the conclusions Engelhardt reaches, but you can't help but be awed by the breadth of his knowledge, the elegance of his arguments, and the sheer audacity of his willingness to take unpopular positions on some of the most important ethical issues in health care and biomedical research. My analysis of the Golden Rule was shaped by this work (though my formulation of its replacement is slightly different from Engelhardt's).

Ruth R. Faden and Tom L. Beauchamp. *A History and Theory of Informed Consent*. New York: Oxford University Press, 1986.

If you want to explore in greater detail the principle of respect for patient autonomy (a broader version of which I call the third principle of ethical intelligence, Respect Others), this is the place to go. Of particular interest is Faden and Beauchamp's discussion of three elements in the continuum of influence: persuasion, manipulation, and coercion.

Harry Frankfurt. *On Truth*. New York: Princeton University Press, 2004.

Frankfurt's previous work, *On Bull——*, is better known, but its twin, *On Truth*, is also worth reading. I've assumed, rather than argued for, the idea that truth in general exists, as does ethical truth in particular, whether such truth is created or discovered. What Frankfurt does so eloquently and concisely is explain why truth should be valued at all. I've taken it as axiomatic that Do No Harm, for example, is an ethical imperative. It may rightly be considered as a premise in any argument about what we ought to do or ought not to do. But it is for experts in epistemology (the branch of philosophy that examines what we know and how we know it) to help us understand why it matters that what I am calling the first principle of ethical intelligence is to be considered true rather than an expression of personal preference. Frankfurt is the best kind of expert: he makes difficult material accessible.

Jostein Gaarder. *Sophie's World*. Translated by Paulette Moller. New York: Farrar, Straus and Giroux, 2007.

Disguised as a children's story about the relationship between inquisitive teenager and a philosopher, *Sophie's World* examines many of the major philosophical questions from pre-Socratic times to the modern era. If you regret not having taken a survey course in philosophy in college, Gaarder's popular novel will help you make up for this gap in your studies.

Daniel Gilbert. *Stumbling on Happiness*. New York: Vintage Books, 2007.

For Aristotle, the quintessential ethical question is, What does it mean to be happy? Gilbert, a professor of psychology at Harvard University, draws upon research in behavioral economics, philosophy, cognitive neuroscience, and psychology to answer Aristotle's question. That answer is consistent with the ethically intelligent life as I have presented it here: a life of interconnectedness, in which we make choices that honor both others and ourselves.

Daniel Goleman. *Emotional Intelligence*. 10th anniversary ed. New York: Bantam Books, 2006.

This is the book that started it all: it gave us a deeper understanding of what it means to be smart. Goleman shows that "book smarts" and a genetic predisposition for doing well academically may not only be insufficient for functioning well in the world; these qualities can be counterproductive. The fully human life must make room for being attuned to how other people are feeling. Goleman's work also prompted me to develop the concept of ethical intelligence. Let's face it: the term *ethics* is off-putting to many because it seems punitive; *ethical intelligence* is inviting and appeals to our better nature. I owe Daniel Goleman an *enormous* debt of gratitude for inspiring the present project, and I can only hope to do for ethics what he has done so marvelously for psychology.

Jon Kabat-Zinn. *Wherever You Go, There You Are*. 10th anniversary
    ed. New York: Hyperion, 2005.

Of the many books on mindfulness meditation out there, this is by far my favorite one. Kabat-Zinn, founding executive director of the Center for Mindfulness in Medicine, Health Care, and Society at the University of Massachusetts Medical School, describes the philosophy of mindfulness in plain, accessible language. While reading the previous sections on anger, multitasking madness, and criticism, you may have wondered, "I know I need to do a better job in these areas, but how can I get started?" The solution may very well be mindfulness. Kabat-Zinn's practice CDs (series 2) are a great way to make this a part of your daily life. They're available at www.mindfulnesstapes.com.

Immanuel Kant. *Groundwork of the Metaphysics of Morals*. Trans-
    lated and edited by Mary Gregor. New York: Cambridge Uni-
    versity Press, 1998.

What I call the third principle of ethical intelligence, Respect Others, is a broader formulation of Beauchamp and Childress's Principle of Respect for Autonomy. It is Immanuel Kant who advanced the notion of autonomy (literally, "self-rule") and stressed the importance of treating human beings as ends in themselves rather than merely as means to an end. Kant's work is notoriously difficult, but *Groundwork* is a good place to begin exploring his contributions to ethics.

Alasdair MacIntyre. *After Virtue: A Study in Moral Theory*. 2nd ed. Notre Dame, IN: University of Notre Dame Press, 1984.

I first learned of this monumental book while a senior at Swarthmore College, when fellow student John Duvivier told our class that it was "piercing the arid air of philosophy" and proposed using it as the basis of his commencement address. That phrase stuck with me, and when I got around to reading it in graduate school at Georgetown, I saw what he meant. MacIntyre argued that ethics had become overly focused on action and neglected character. In calling for a renewed appreciation for excellence of character, *After Virtue* is one of those rare books that will prompt you to see the world — and your life — in a completely new way.

Jeffrey Moses. *Oneness: Great Principles Shared by All Religions*. New York: Ballantine Books, 2002.

Do ethical values vary from religion to religion? Not at the most fundamental level, as Jeffrey Moses illustrates here. He cites specific textual references in Hinduism, Buddhism, Christianity, Judaism, Islam, and other traditions that call upon the faithful to tell the truth, avoid harming others, and follow all of the other forms of right conduct I've discussed in this book. It's true that each faith has a unique way of presenting their calls to action. With respect to loving one another, for example, Judaism says, "Thou shalt love thy neighbor as thyself." This idea is expressed in Christianity this way: "A new commandment I give to you, that you love one another even as I have loved you." In Islam, it is, "No one is a believer until he loves for his neighbor, and for his brother, what he loves for himself." The articulations may be different, but the core ideas, which I'm calling the five principles of ethical intelligence, are the bedrock of every religious and spiritual tradition the world has ever known.

Plato. *The Republic*. In *The Collected Dialogues of Plato, Including the Letters*. Edited by Edith Hamilton and Huntington Cairns. New York: Princeton University Press, 2005.

Whatever preconceived notions (that is, prejudices) you may have about philosophy, Plato will dispel them all. The polar opposite of dry, boring academic exercises in pseudo-intellectualism, Platonic dialogues crackle with wit, wisdom, and excitement. They read like great screenplays about the things that matter most. You may wish to start with *The Republic*, a work that can be read as politics, philosophy, or simply great literature. This is where you'll find the allegory of the cave, a metaphor for levels of knowledge. I fell in love with philosophy in high school because of this book, and it may cast a similar spell on you, too.

Dr. Seuss. "The Zax." In *The Sneetches and Other Stories*. New York: Random House, 1961.

Stubbornness is ethically unintelligent because it can prevent us from doing things that are beneficial to ourselves and others. This wonderful story illustrates how stubbornness is self-defeating. A north-going Zax and a south-going Zax meet, and each refuses to budge. They remain firmly planted while life unfolds around them, presumably for the rest of their lives. Yes, it's hard to swallow one's pride, or admit defeat, or simply defer to others; but "The Zax" shows why it's in our own interest to do so.

Bruce Weinstein. *Is It Still Cheating If I Don't Get Caught?* New York: Roaring Brook Press, 2009.

When *Rolling Stone* magazine asks rock musicians to list their five or ten favorite albums, one or two inevitably are their own work, which suggests an appalling lack of modesty and humility on their part. At the risk of being accused of the same thing, I feel compelled to mention my previous book here, simply because it takes the five principles of ethical intelligence (which I call "Life Principles" there) and shows tweens and teens how to apply them in their own lives.

David Zinczenko and Matt Goulding. *Eat This, Not That!: The No-Diet Weight Loss Solution.* Emmaus, PA: Rodale Books, 2010.

I explained in chapter 10 why it is ethically intelligent to eat healthfully. It is extraordinarily difficult to do this, especially with so many temptations everywhere you look. Updated yearly, this delightful book accomplishes the near-impossible feat of providing valuable information about good and bad nutrition in an entertaining way. Each page has detailed color photos of both gastronomic nightmares and daydreams. You'll be appalled when you see how much fat, sodium, and carbohydrates are tucked away in certain restaurant meals, compared with some of the healthier choices on the menus. Equipped with this knowledge, you'll be better prepared to make ethically intelligent decisions when you go out to eat. Other books in the series include *Drink This, Not That!, Cook This, Not That!,* and *Eat This, Not That! for Kids.* I highly recommend them all.

MOVIES AND TV SHOWS

Why are we so fascinated with stories about evildoers? What is it about the adventures of people doing the wrong things that keep us so entertained? I'm not a psychologist, but I suspect the reason has something to do with the fantasy that many of us have of being completely free to do whatever we want, whenever we want, and with (or to) whomever we want. In other words, these stories portray characters who are concerned first and foremost with satisfying their own desires, no matter what the consequences are. Who wouldn't want to live this way, free of the constraints imposed by the principles of ethical intelligence?

Consider the protagonists, for example, in *The Godfather* (and *The Godfather, Part II*), *Scarface*, *GoodFellas*, and *The Sopranos*. It may seem that Michael Corleone, Tony Montana, Henry Hill, and Tony Soprano enjoy a kind of freedom that the rest of us only dream about. But if you actually look at what happens to these characters, they all end up worse off as a result of their lifestyle. Whatever thrill existed during their rise to power gives way to fear, isolation, and murder. On their face, these stories — and plenty of others like them — celebrate or glamorize the life of gangsters. But if you step back and consider the wide arc of each one, it's clear that these are moral fables, or tales that vividly portray the dangers of living an immoral life. Their message is not an encouragement to live the way their characters do but just the opposite: when you focus primarily or exclusively on your own needs and desires, and you are willing to do whatever it takes to satisfy them, you will pay a heavy price and might not be able to undo the damage you have caused by your choices.

Because these stories are violent and filled with graphic language and sexuality, they are not for everyone. But make no mistake about it: only ethically unintelligent persons would choose to model themselves after these wiseguys or think their way of life is cool.

Albert Maysles, codirector of such documentary films as *Salesman*, *The Gates*, and the Oscar-nominated *LaLee's Kin*, has bemoaned the current state of cinema and, by extension, all of popular culture. "They're stories about bad people doing bad things to other bad people," he said, and it's hard not to agree with him. But once upon a time in America, there was a TV program that showed how good, not how evil, we can be to one another. That program was *The Andy Griffith Show* (created by Sheldon Leonard). "A Medal for Opie," an episode from season 2, which I discussed in the context of the fourth principle of ethical intelligence, is but one of many outstanding examples of how to put the five principles of ethical intelligence into action. It's possible to teach a wide-ranging course in ethics using only *The Andy Griffith Show*, and at least one college professor I know of is doing just that (not to mention the countless numbers of Sunday schools that do the same). And it's not just for us old-timers. I showed a clip to eighth graders, who sat in rapt attention throughout. There has never been, and probably will never be, a TV show as consistently good — in every sense — as *The Andy Griffith Show*.

Here are some recommendations for other films and TV programs that will deepen your appreciation of ethical intelligence. For ease of reference, I'm categorizing these works by the principle each illustrates so well.

Do No Harm

The Red Balloon (written and directed by Albert Lamorisse) and *Spirited Away* (written and directed by Hayao Miyazaki) are two cinematic gems. The central conflict in each is resolved nonviolently. Why are there so few films like this for children and even fewer for adults?

Make Things Better

In *Late Spring* (written by Kazuo Hirotsu, Kogo Noda, and Yasujiro Ozu; directed by Yasujiro Ozu), a father and his adult daughter live together in a small Japanese town after World War II. He wants her to get married; she wants to live the rest of her life with him. Does the father ultimately do the right thing to make things better for his daughter? There's much room for debate. If you've never seen a film by Ozu, you're in for a treat. If you've seen this before, it's worth another look.

Respect Others

Confidentiality

Rear Window (written by John Michael Hayes, based on the short story "It Had to Be Murder" by Cornell Woolrich; directed by Alfred Hitchcock) is an exploration of what it means to be a good neighbor. The duty to respect a person's right to privacy should be infringed to protect the well-being of others, right? What's James Stewart's character doing spying on his neighbors to begin with? This magnum opus invites repeated viewings and a lively discussion of these issues.

Truth Telling

It might seem that the obvious choice here is *A Few Good Men* (written by Aaron Sorkin; directed by Rob Reiner) with its oft-repeated line "You can't handle the truth!" But I'll recommend instead *The Invention of Lying* (written and directed by Ricky Gervais and Matthew Robinson), if only for the opening sequence, which perfectly illustrates why it is ethically unintelligent to tell the truth, the whole truth, and nothing but the truth in every social situation.

Promise Keeping

Is there anything more boring in movies than stories about adultery? Still, the best way to show the value of being faithful to one's partner may be through narratives that show the consequences of infidelity and how difficult it is to keep the ruse going. I'm thinking here of scenes from *The Ice Storm* (written by James Schamus, based on the novel by Rick Moody; directed by Ang Lee) and *The Kids Are All Right* (written by Lisa Cholodenko and Stuart Blumberg; directed by Lisa Cholodenko). The discovery of infidelity is made through small observations: a new scent on a spouse's skin, the presence of another person's hair on a hairbrush. Something always gives the cheater away, no matter how hard he or she tries to keep it under wraps.

Be Fair

Although a bit dated and simplistic, *12 Angry Men* (written by Reginald Rose; directed by Sidney Lumet) is still one of the best examples of how prejudice in the jury box contaminates everything it touches but can be vanquished by one juror's dogged commitment to objectivity and fairness.

In chapter 9, I discuss three examples of ethically unintelligent behavior by customers of local businesses. A comic example of this is "The Ida Funkhouser Roadside Memorial," an episode from season 6 of *Curb Your Enthusiasm* (created by Larry David). An ice cream store patron abuses her sampling privileges, but her lack of ethical intelligence is matched, and even trumped, by another customer's response to this small injustice.[1] We see later in the episode how that response is self-defeating, reinforcing the central theme of this book: ethically intelligent choices increase your chances of getting what you want, and ethically unintelligent choices do the opposite.

Be Loving

Putting aside films and TV shows about romantic love, with what are we left? If what we're seeking is a story that makes you want to do good things for people, it's hard to do better than *Groundhog Day* (written by Danny Rubin and Harold Ramis; directed by Harold Ramis). Through a quirk in the space-time continuum, a self-absorbed blowhard is forced to live the same day over and over again and gradually learns to care about more than just himself.

The film may be better known for its time-travel implications than for what the movie itself is really all about: benefiting yourself by bettering the lives of others. It's time to revisit this tale and take its lessons to heart.

For TV, one program towers above them all. It ran on CBS for five seasons in the 1960s and told the story of a simple man who sees only the good in people. No matter what adversity comes his way, his belief that human beings are fundamentally decent is unshakable. The show is a brilliant example of how ethical intelligence doesn't require years of formal education and of why the fifth principle of ethical intelligence may be the most valuable one of all. The show I'm talking about is, of course, *Gomer Pyle, U.S.M.C.* (created by Aaron Ruben). Don't be fooled by its slapstick elements; at its core, this sitcom is a modern-day morality play about the deepest, most meaningful sense of love.

What books, short stories, films, and TV shows that bring the concept of ethical intelligence to life do you like? I'd love to know. Contact me through my website, TheEthicsGuy.com.

Acknowledgments

I owe a colossal debt of gratitude to Tom L. Beauchamp and James F. Childress for their pioneering work, *Principles of Biomedical Ethics*, 6th ed. (New York: Oxford University Press, 2008). What I'm calling the first four principles of ethical intelligence are a reiteration of what Beauchamp and Childress call the principles of nonmaleficence, beneficence, respect for autonomy, and justice. What I refer to as principle 5, or the duty to be loving, is simply another way of presenting the ethics of care that Beauchamp and Childress have adopted from virtue ethics. All I've done, really, is to translate Beauchamp and Childress's philosophically rich ideas into terms that may be more accessible to those who live and work outside academia. Thus nonmaleficence becomes Do No Harm, beneficence becomes Make Things Better, and so forth. I'm also applying these principles beyond the world of health care since I believe they provide the foundation not just for physicians, nurses, dentists, pharmacists, and researchers but for everyone. But I can in no way claim the principles of ethical intelligence as my own. I was extremely fortunate to be able to study with Tom L. Beauchamp when I was a graduate student at Georgetown University, and my work would not be possible without his and James F. Childress's contributions to ethical theory.

During my first four years of writing an ethics column for what is now Bloomberg Businessweek online, I was blessed to have Patricia O'Connell as my editor. Patricia is that rare literary professional: an editor who considers her mission to be helping writers make the strongest possible arguments rather than imposing her point of view on the work. Reasonable people can disagree about many things, and not once did Patricia ever tell me that I was wrong. But she often told me — and rightly so — that I wasn't making a convincing case for whatever position I was arguing for or against. It was through Patricia's careful guidance that I developed many of the ideas in this book, and I am grateful to her for helping me express these ideas as clearly as possible and support them with the strongest possible arguments.

I have been lucky to work with another fabulous editor, Jason Gardner of New World Library. His comments on an earlier draft helped me to clarify muddled points, strengthen arguments, and provide a more satisfying structure to the book. May all writers have an editor who is such a joy to work with! For the past year and a half, I've road tested the concept of ethical intelligence thanks to Michael Frick, who manages my speaking engagements through his company, the Core Speakers Agency. My heartfelt thanks for a job well done also go to my literary agent, Nena Madonia, and to Jan Miller, both of Dupree/Miller Associates.

Jeff Clarkson helped me navigate through some of the tricky legal waters that this project required before going full-sail with it, and Mark Colucci went far beyond his duties as copyeditor and suggested many substantive changes that were most valuable.

Once again, my colleague and friend, Robert Timko, who recently retired as professor and chair of the Department of Philosophy and interim dean of arts and sciences at Mansfield University, reviewed the manuscript from a philosophical perspective and offered numerous helpful suggestions for improving it. Diana A.

Goldberg, executive director of SungateKids, a nonprofit children's advocacy agency in Denver, signed off on my discussion of the legal rights of children in chapter 2, which is great because she is an expert in this area, and I am not.

David Maltsberger, associate professor of biblical studies and archaeology at Baptist University of the Americas, validated the cultural claims I made about several religious traditions; how nice to benefit from the wisdom and kindness of a fine fellow who was in my fifth-grade class at Harmony Hills Elementary School in San Antonio, Texas, many years ago. Dr. Omar Manejwala and Mr. Chuck Rice took time from their busy schedules at Hazelden in Center City, Minnesota, to review the story about the alcoholic boss and to answer several questions I had about addiction and recovery. Meg Owen helped me organize my voluminous files and continues to fight against the entropy that inevitably creeps into my office workspace (but for which I take full responsibility, in keeping with the guidelines for apologizing with ethical intelligence).

Quiet and solitude are two essential components of the writer's life, and my beloved bride, Kristen Bancroft, was extraordinarily generous in giving me the gift of both of these valuable commodities when I needed them. But wait! There's more! Kristen also reviewed the entire manuscript and helped me make every chapter better. It is a blessing to be married to someone who is so brilliant, loving, and kind.

What a loving family I have in Sheila, Liz, and Rachel Weinstein (mother and sisters, respectively), Carlee and Sammy Daylor (niece and nephew), and my terrific mother-in-law, Judy Bancroft. They show me, on a regular basis, what it means to live by the fifth principle of ethical intelligence. Although my father isn't with us any longer, I am beholden to him and my mom for teaching me ethics and for having lively discussions about ethical issues with my sisters and me during most of our family dinners.

My grandfather used to say, "If at the end of your life, you can count all of your true friends on one hand, then you have done well." Although I'm not close to the end of my life (I hope), I can say that I have been blessed with four terrific friends who have been on this journey with me for many, many years. They are Edward Askinazi, Jeffrey L. Clarkson, William Wells Hood, and B. David Joffe, to whom I have dedicated this book with respect and gratitude.

Notes

Chapter 1: Introducing the Principles

1. Jeffrey Moses, *Oneness: Great Principles Shared by All Religions* (New York: Ballantine Books, 2002).
2. Daniel Goleman, *Emotional Intelligence*, 10th anniversary ed. (New York: Bantam Books, 2006).

Chapter 2: The Five Principles of Ethical Intelligence

1. Terrence O'Brien, "Unfunny Amber Alert Hoax Spreads Via Twitter and Text Message," Switched, February 14, 2009, http://www.switched.com/2009/02/14/unfunny-amber-alert-hoax-spreads-via-twitter-and-text-message.
2. It's not just doing nothing versus doing something that distinguishes Do No Harm from Prevent Harm. Do No Harm usually speaks to harm that you yourself might cause; in Prevent Harm, the harm emanates from somewhere (or someone) else.
3. There are, of course, limits to what you should be expected to do simply because someone asks you to do it. For example, businesses have no obligation to honor unfair demands that customers make. I explore this in chapter 8.
4. George Carlin, *George Carlin: It's Bad for Ya*, directed by Rocco Urbisci (Orland Park, IL: MPI Home Video, 2008), DVD. This performance is also available on CD at www.laugh.com and as an MP3 download from many online retailers. Be warned that some of this material contains language and points of view that you may find offensive. But because his

discussion of rights is relevant here, the material is readily available, and many people appear to share his beliefs, I felt it would be useful to cite it.

5. International Centre for Missing & Exploited Children, "Child Pornography Is Not a Crime in Most Countries," Progress Report, Summer 2006, accessed March 30, 2011, www.icmec.org/en_Xi/pdf/Summer Newsletter2006formatted.pdf.

6. Ibid.

7. Saying, "I wasn't aware of what I was doing," isn't a reasonable defense against breaches of confidentiality. To be ethically intelligent means, in part, to be mindful of one's actions. One resource (discussed in the appendix) for enhancing mindfulness is Jon Kabat-Zinn, *Wherever You Go, There You Are*, 10th anniversary ed. (New York: Hyperion, 2005).

8. This speaks to what Aristotle calls *phronesis*, or practical wisdom. A tuneful explanation of the importance of practical wisdom in everyday life can be found in the song "The Gambler," made popular by Kenny Rogers. For more on Aristotle, see Aristotle, *Nicomachean Ethics*, trans. Martin Ostwald (Indianapolis: Bobbs-Merrill, 1962). To find out when you can hear Kenny Rogers sing "The Gambler" in person, see http:// kennyrogers.musiccitynetworks.com.

9. Ben Sisario, "Dr Pepper and Rocker in a War of Hype," *New York Times*, November 26, 2008, www.nytimes.com/2008/11/27/arts/music /27pepp.html.

10. Whether it's ethical for a band to keep its name after losing all but one of its original members is a matter for another discussion.

11. This idea comes from Immanuel Kant, whose work I discuss briefly in the appendix.

12. I'm grateful to Dianne Trumbull for helping me to see "A Medal for Opie" is about discipline, not punishment.

13. In a sense, this formulation of the principle of fairness is a dodge. What, one might ask, *is* due to others? The correct answer to this question is, it depends. That is, what is due to others depends on the context. In some situations, it is based on need. (For example, the college-bound child of poor parents has a greater need for, and thus a greater claim to, a grant than the child of wealthy parents does.) In other situations, what is due is based on the order in which others make a claim — the "first come, first served" rule of fairness. (It's not unfair for the second caller to a radio station to be

denied a pair of tickets to see Lady Gaga if the disc jockey announces, "Be the first caller, and get a pair of tickets to see Lady Gaga.")

For a more thorough analysis of this complex topic, see Tom L. Beauchamp and James F. Childress, *Principles of Biomedical Ethics*, 6th ed. (New York: Oxford University Press, 2008).

14. Punishment and discipline are concepts that merit their own book. Briefly, punishment has several possible goals, some of which conflict; discipline is more limited in scope. There is probably more agreement about the purpose of discipline than about the purpose of punishment. To discipline someone (your child, an employee) is to help that person see the error of his or her ways and to get him or her back on track. To discipline may also be to send a message to others (the child's siblings, other employees) that such behavior is not to be tolerated. Punishment can include discipline but it need not, and for some extreme forms of behavior — pedophilia, for example — rehabilitation may not even be possible. In these cases, and even in less extreme forms of errant conduct (fraud, robbery, identity theft), the goal may simply be retribution. By committing certain wrongful acts, one owes a debt to society, and some rights may legitimately be taken away temporarily or permanently, such as through incarceration.

Whether you have to discipline a direct report for sending an inappropriate email or you're on a jury deliberating about the just punishment for a white-collar crook, ethical intelligence calls upon you to moderate your feelings. Only then is it possible to discipline or punish fairly.

15. The ethically intelligent response to being discriminated against may also be to take legal action. It depends on a variety of factors. I am not an attorney and am not qualified to offer legal advice. I'm merely suggesting that there is a range of possible responses to being on the receiving end of an injustice, and not all of them are ethically intelligent.

16. Erich Fromm, *The Art of Loving*, trans. Marion Hausner Pauk, 50th anniversary ed. (New York: Harper Perennial, 2006).

17. Dale Carnegie, *How to Win Friends and Influence People*, rev. ed. (New York: Pocket Books, 1981).

18. Jim Harter and Sangeeta Agrawal, "Workers in Bad Jobs Have Worse Wellbeing Than Jobless," Gallup, March 30, 2011, www.gallup.com/poll/146867/Workers-Bad-Jobs-Worse-Wellbeing-Jobless.aspx.

Chapter 3: Revisiting the Quiz

1. Emily Bryson York, "Kellogg to Drop Olympian Phelps," Ad Age, February 5, 2009, http://adage.com/article/news/kellogg-drop-olympian-michael-phelps-bong-photo/134363.

2. I say that it's "almost" impossible to erase Internet communications, because there are businesses that — for a price — can remove some of them for you. The service isn't cheap; one "reputation management company" charges celebrities, politicians, and high-level executives between $5,000 and $10,000 per month. Nick Bilton, "Erasing the Digital Past," *New York Times*, April 1, 2011, www.nytimes.com/2011/04/03/fashion/03reputation.html.

3. Aristotle, *Nicomachean Ethics*, trans. Martin Ostwald (Indianapolis: Bobbs-Merrill, 1962). The "treat like cases alike" rule is traced to Aristotle's discussion of distributive justice in book 5.

Chapter 4: Ten Questions about Ethics and Ethical Intelligence

1. Bruce Weinstein, "The Possibility of Ethical Expertise" (doctoral dissertation, Georgetown University, 1989). I argued that there are two kinds of expertise: epistemic and performative. The first kind concerns people who are experts by virtue of what they *know* (hence the designation "epistemic," which comes from the Greek word for knowledge); the second refers to people who are experts by virtue of what they *do*. One kind of expertise does not entail the other. Robert De Niro is one of the greatest screen actors of all time, but he is almost completely at a loss to explain how he was able to create such memorable performances as Travis Bickle in *Taxi Driver*, Jake LaMotta in *Raging Bull*, and Rupert Pupkin in *The King of Comedy*. The distinction between epistemic and performative expertise has profound implications in ethics: someone can do good things but be unable to give anything more than a cursory explanation of why he or she does them. An example I cited in my dissertation was Mother Teresa's appearance on William F. Buckley Jr.'s TV program *Firing Line*. Buckley wanted to know why a person would dedicate her life to serving the poor, but all Mother Teresa could say was, "It's God's will." By the same token, a person can be a scholar of ethical theory yet unfaithful to his wife and dishonest on his income tax returns. Still, when we want to know what we should do and why we

should do it, there are good reasons to turn to ethics experts (in the epistemic sense) for help.

Chapter 5: Plays Well with Others

1. Sammy Hagar with Joel Selvin, *Red: My Uncensored Life in Rock* (New York: It Books, 2011), 91–93.

2. See Jeffrey Moses, *Oneness: Great Principles Shared by All Religions* (New York: Ballantine Books, 2002).

3. Created by Buddy Ruskin, this TV series ran on ABC from 1968 to 1973. See "The Mod Squad," Internet Movie Database, accessed April 10, 2011, www.imdb.com/title/tt0062589; and "The Mod Squad," *Wikipedia*, last modified March 29, 2011, http://en.wikipedia.org/wiki/The_Mod_Squad.

4. I'm not taking a position about whether aesthetic judgments are objective or subjective, because it's not relevant to the point I'm making about the ethics of having political conversations in the office. Even if *Citizen Kane* is truly a better film than *Dude, Where's My Car?* (and there is much evidence to support this claim), arguments about cinema generally don't have the same negative consequences as those about political issues and campaigns. If I say that *Ernest Saves Christmas* is a cinematic masterpiece, you may think I'm strange (and you'd have good reason to think so), but this probably wouldn't affect our working relationship. However, if you and I are on opposite sides of a controversial political issue and this becomes fodder for discussion at work, problems between us may very well occur.

5. Remy Melina, "Why Were Red M&M's Discontinued for a Decade?," Life's Little Mysteries, February 10, 2011, www.lifeslittlemysteries.com/why-were-red-mms-discontinued-for-a-decade-1339.

6. Since red M&M's were discontinued due to health concerns related to the dye used on them, it might appear that a discussion about that issue could be just as volatile as one about closing a manufacturing plant. But they're not commensurable issues because a person would have to have eaten an awful lot of M&M's for there to be a serious risk to his or her well-being.

7. Harper Lee, *To Kill a Mockingbird* (New York: Harper Perennial Modern Classics, 2006), p. 33.

8. A commitment to bringing out the best in others is the foundation of servant leadership. See Robert K. Greenleaf, *Servant Leadership: A Journey*

into the Nature of Legitimate Power and Greatness, 25th anniversary ed. (Mahwah, NJ: Paulist Press, 2007).

9. Don Miguel Ruiz, *The Four Agreements: A Practical Guide to Personal Freedom* (San Rafael, CA: Amber-Allen, 1997), 47ff.

10. Mark Twain, *Mark Twain's Notebook*, quoted in Barbara Schmidt, "Cheerfulness," Mark Twain Quotations, Newspaper Collections & Related Resources, accessed May 4, 2011, www.twainquotes.com/Cheer fulness.html.

Chapter 6: Are You a Good Leader?

1. Thich Nhat Hanh, *Anger: Wisdom for Cooling the Flames* (New York: Riverhead Books, 2002).

2. Matt Hines, "Facing Digital Realities, Kodak to Trim Staff," CNET News, January 22, 2004, http://news.cnet.com/Facing-digital-realities, -Kodak-to-trim-staff/2100-1047_3-5145259.html.

3. B. David Joffe, personal communication with author, March 31, 2011.

4. This is a good example of a rule that is both legal and ethical.

Chapter 7: You're Not the Boss of Me!
Oh, Wait a Second — You Are

1. To speak of prudence is to recognize the role that virtue plays in the ethically intelligent life. In the appendix, I identify several important works about virtue, and I intend to explore this crucial topic in a subsequent volume about ethical intelligence.

2. For more examples of Elizabethan-era insults, consult the handy chart in Suzanne L. Gordon, "The Elizabethan Insult and Curses of an Elizabethan Nature or, How to Cuss Like an Elizabethan Sailor," accessed April 10, 2011, www.museangel.net/insult.html; and "Elizabethan Oaths, Curses, and Insults," accessed April 10, 2011, www.renfaire.com/Language /insults.html (which also contains a useful bibliography on the topic).

3. See Jan Hoffman, "A Girl's Nude Photo, and Altered Lives," *New York Times*, March 24, 2011, www.nytimes.com/2011/03/27/us/27sexting. html, for an example of the harsh consequences of anonymous Internet communication and how the revelation of the sender's identity made him rethink what he had done.

4. Tina Fey, *Bossypants* (New York: Reagan Arthur Books, 2011).

5. Janet Maslin, "Tina Fey Is Greek and Also Teutonic, but She Isn't a Troll," *New York Times*, April 3, 2011, www.nytimes.com/2011/04/04/books/bossypants-by-tina-fey-review.html.

6. Omar Manejwala, personal communication with author, April 1, 2011.

7. National Survey on Drug Use and Health, https://nsduhweb.rti.org.

8. Wendy Lee, "Hazelden Lines Up New Help for Attorney Addicts," *Star Tribune*, January 6, 2011, www.startribune.com/local/east/113050504.html?elr=KArks7PYDiaK7DUqEiaDUiD3aPc:_Yyc:aUoD3aPc:_27EQU,.

9. Chuck Rice, personal communication with author, April 1, 2011.

Chapter 8: Stand by Me

1. For more about the differences between shareholders and stakeholders, see "Shareholder," *Wikipedia*, last modified March 15, 2011, http://en.wikipedia.org/wiki/Shareholder; and "Stakeholder," *Wikipedia*, last modified March 3, 2011, http://en.wikipedia.org/wiki/Stakeholder.

2. Asking someone, "Why did you do *x*?" can put him or her on the defensive. Saying instead, "Help me to understand this," is more likely to get results, and it does so in a nonthreatening way. I learned this technique from Kellogg Fellow Darlyne Bailey, dean and professor of the Graduate School of Social Work and Social Research at Bryn Mawr College.

3. Miguel Helft, "Jobs Takes Sick Leave at Apple Again, Stirring Questions," *New York Times*, January 17, 2011, www.nytimes.com/2011/01/18/technology/18apple.html.

4. Maureen Salamon, "The Hidden Illnesses of Presidents," MyHealthNewsDaily, February 17, 2011, www.myhealthnewsdaily.com/illnesses-of-presidents-secret-surgeries-110217-1184. Salamon quotes Robert Lahita, chairman of the Department of Medicine at Newark Beth Israel Medical Center, who has studied the subject. A summary of Lahita's research can be found in "Hidden Illnesses of U.S. Presidents Discussed by Chairman of the Department of Medicine at Newark Beth Israel Medical Center," Newark Beth Israel Medical Center, January 3, 2011, www.saintbarnabas.com/hospitals/newark_beth_israel/press/2011/lahita_president_illness.html.

5. The ethics of outsourcing *any* job is important to consider but lies

beyond the scope of this discussion. I plan to tackle this knotty subject in a future work.

6. Ilan Brat and Jared Favole, "Food Makers Warned on Claims," *Wall Street Journal*, March 4, 2010, http://online.wsj.com/article/SB100014 24052748703862704575099950193636906.html.

7. Jeffrey M. Jones, "Nurses Top Honesty and Ethics List for 11th Year," Gallup, December 3, 2010, www.gallup.com/poll/145043/Nurses-Top -Honesty-Ethics-List-11-Year.aspx. See the actual 2010 survey results in "Honesty/Ethics in Professions," Gallup, November 19–21, 2010, www .gallup.com/poll/1654/Honesty-Ethics-Professions.aspx.

8. This statement assumes that people who engage in unethical business practices are aware that what they're doing is wrong but do it anyway. Yet, as we all know, there are some people in this category for whom the concept of ethics isn't even on the radar.

9. Sheryl Gay Stolberg, Shaila Dewan, and Brian Stelter, "With Apology, Fired Official Is Offered a New Job," *New York Times*, July 21, 2010, www.nytimes.com/2010/07/22/us/politics/22sherrod.html.

10. Maureen Miller, "Evening Buzz: An Apology for Sherrod," Anderson Cooper 360, July 21, 2010, http://ac360.blogs.cnn.com/2010/07/21 /evening-buzz-an-apology-for-sherrod.

11. In the interests of full disclosure, I will add that Shirley Sherrod and I were in the same fellowship program, sponsored by the W. K. Kellogg Foundation, at the same time.

12. It is beyond the scope of this book to investigate the issue of ethical relativism — the belief that there is no objective truth about ethical judgments. With the example of the thieving financial consultant, I've provided at least one counterargument to ethical relativism, but there is obviously much more to be said about the matter. However, I suspect that the reason you're reading this book (assuming that you're doing so of your own free will and not because it has been assigned to you) is because you already buy into the notion that at least some ethical judgments are true or false.

13. Kirsten Korosec, "Gulf Oil Spill: BP CEO Hayward Just Can't Help Blaming Someone Else," BNET, April 29, 2010, www.bnet.com/blog /clean-energy/gulf-oil-spill-bp-ceo-hayward-just-can-8217t-help -blaming-someone-else/1717.

Chapter 9: We Are Family

1. Elizabeth Mendes, "Americans Worry More about Lack of Money Than Job Loss," Gallup, January 20, 2011, www.gallup.com/poll/145730 /Americans-Worry-Lack-Money-Job-Loss.aspx.

2. Stacey Standish (spokesperson, Bureau of Labor Statistics, U.S. Department of Labor), personal communication with author, March 31, 2011.

3. Michael Gates Gill, *How Starbucks Saved My Life: A Son of Privilege Learns to Live Like Everyone Else* (New York: Gotham Books, 2007).

4. Barron H. Lerner, "A Life-Changing Case for Doctors in Training," *New York Times*, March 2, 2009, www.nytimes.com/2009/03/03/health /03zion.html. I am not related to the resident involved in the case who bears my surname.

5. In the United States, the right to a vacation is an ethical one, not a legal one. According to B. David Joffe (personal communication with author, May 10, 2010), "There is no federal law that mandates the provision of vacation leave or payment for such leave for employees in the private sector. Certain public sector employees and employees under a government contract may be entitled to paid vacation leave." For more information, see "Vacation Leave," U.S. Department of Labor, accessed April 10, 2011, www.dol.gov/dol/topic/workhours/vacation_leave.htm.

   By an ethical right to a vacation, I mean that your employer ought to allow you to take time off every year, whether or not the organization has a legal responsibility to do this. Ideally, this means you should be paid while on vacation, but at the very least, you should not be penalized or stigmatized for taking a break. The ethical right to a vacation thus refers to any time away from work, paid or unpaid, for restorative purposes.

6. Jeanne Sahadi, "Who Gets the Most (and Least) Vacation," CNNMoney .com, June 14, 2007, http://money.cnn.com/2007/06/12/pf/vacation _days_worldwide.

7. Barbara Mikkelson and David P. Mikkelson, "The Secret Words," Snopes.com, last modified January 6, 2007, www.snopes.com/radiotv /tv/grouchocigar.asp.

8. This is a reference to the surprisingly delightful film written by Kevin James and Nick Bakay and directed by Steve Carr. A flight attendant once announced to my fellow passengers and me, "The movie this

afternoon will be *Mall Cop*, starring Paul Blart." But it's actually Kevin James who plays the lead role.

9. Bruce Weinstein, "If Borders Goes Under, Who Will Be to Blame?," *New York Times*, February 26, 2011, www.nytimes.com/2011/02/27 /opinion/lweb27borders.html.

Chapter 10: If I Am Not for Myself, Who Will Be?

1. Matt Richtel, "Your Brain on Computers: Attached to Technology and Paying a Price," *New York Times*, June 6, 2010, www.nytimes.com /2010/06/07/technology/07brain.html.

2. Edward M. Hallowell, *CrazyBusy: Overstretched, Overbooked, and About to Snap! Strategies for Coping in a World Gone ADD* (New York: Ballantine Books, 2006), quoted in Alina Tugend, "Multitasking Can Make You Lose...Um...Focus," *New York Times*, October 24, 2008, www .nytimes.com/2008/10/25/business/yourmoney/25shortcuts.html.

3. Matt Richtel, "In Study, Texting Lifts Crash Risk by Large Margin," *New York Times*, July 27, 2009, www.nytimes.com/2009/07/28 /technology/28texting.html. Lest you think that the twenty-three-fold increase in crashes applies only to *truck drivers* who text, Richtel reports the following: "Even though trucks take longer to stop and are less maneuverable than cars, the findings generally applied to all drivers, who tend to exhibit the same behaviors as the more than 100 truckers studied, the researchers said."

4. "Texting While Driving," *Wikipedia*, last modified April 10, 2011, http://en.wikipedia.org/wiki/Texting_while_driving.

5. Bowman, special ethics counsel for the law firm Burns White, and Jackson Kelly Professor of Law Emeritus at West Virginia University, makes this distinction in the time-management seminars he teaches. I had the pleasure of taking one of his seminars while I was a professor at the West Virginia University Health Sciences Center.

6. Robert Timko, who until recently was chair of the Department of Philosophy at Mansfield University, made this observation: "I remain continually dismayed by the number of students who feel they need to text friends while in class instead of participating in the discussion. In an interesting way, technology should remind us of Plato's cave. It may not be fire casting shadows, but what we get from the computer or the cell phone or the iPod is an image nonetheless. It is taking us away from

what is real and what is valuable." Personal communication with author, March 27, 2011. For more about Plato's allegory of the cave, see Plato, *The Republic,* in *The Collected Dialogues of Plato, Including the Letters,* ed. Edith Hamilton and Huntington Cairns (New York: Princeton University Press, 2005).

Fran Liebowitz makes a similar observation in Martin Scorsese's 2011 documentary *Public Speaking,* originally broadcast on HBO. A synopsis and trailer of the film are available at www.hbo.com/documentaries /public-speaking/index.html.

7. The software is available at http://macfreedom.com. I have no financial stake in the company; I'm just glad it exists. It certainly helped me focus while I wrote this book.

8. Neil Postman, *Amusing Ourselves to Death: Public Discourse in the Age of Show Business,* 20th anniversary ed. (New York: Penguin Books, 2005). Written well before the age of the Internet and cell phones, Postman's book is still relevant.

9. Carl Kruger, "Rise in 'Pedestrian Distraction' Prompts Renewed Call for Sen. Carl Kruger's iPod Bill," New York State Senate website, January 25, 2011, www.nysenate.gov/press-release/rise-pedestrian-distraction -prompts-renewed-call-sen-carl-kruger-s-ipod-bill. See also Taylor Behrendt and Amanda Vanallen, "Distracted Pedestrians Might Have to Pay Up," ABCNews.com, January 25, 2011, http://abcnews.go.com /US/texting-walking-risk/story?id=12756091.

10. "ABC America This Morning: Woman Falls into Fountain While Texting," YouTube video, 0:52, posted by "repeteproductions," January 18, 2011, www.youtube.com/watch?v=bGpVpsaItpU.

11. Charles McGrath, "The Afterlife of Stieg Larsson," *New York Times,* May 20, 2010, www.nytimes.com/2010/05/23/magazine/23Larsson-t .html.

12. David Zinczenko and Matt Goulding, *Eat This, Not That!: The No-Diet Weight Loss Solution* (Emmaus, PA: Rodale Books, 2010), 70.

13. Quoted in Joanne Silberner, "100 Years Ago, Exercise Was Blended into Daily Life," National Public Radio transcript, June 7, 2010, www.npr .org/templates/story/story.php?storyId=127525702.

14. Mayo Clinic staff, "Exercise: 7 Benefits of Regular Physical Activity," MayoClinic.com, July 25, 2009, www.mayoclinic.com/health/exercise /HQ01676.

15. Thich Nhat Hanh, *Anger: Wisdom for Cooling the Flames* (New York: Riverhead Books, 2002).

16. Chris Isidore, "Job Losses: Worst in 5 Years," CNNMoney.com, March 14, 2008, http://money.cnn.com/2008/03/07/news/economy/jobs_february.

17. "Holmes and Rahe Stress Scale," *Wikipedia*, last modified February 1, 2011, http://en.wikipedia.org/wiki/Holmes_and_Rahe_stress_scale.

18. Harvey Mackay, *We Got Fired!...And It's the Best Thing That Ever Happened to Us* (New York: Ballantine Books, 2004).

19. ThinkExist.com, accessed July 1, 2011, http://thinkexist.com/quotation/he_who_angers_you_conquers_you/204255.html.

Appendix

1. For a brief analysis of this scene, see "The Ethics Guy on 'Curb Your Enthusiasm,'" YouTube video, 1:47, posted by "TheEthicsGuy" [Bruce Weinstein], May 18, 2010, www.youtube.com/watch?v=Q_CPQ2xqAfc.

Index

About the Author

D r. Bruce Weinstein, The Ethics Guy®, has a simple purpose in life: to show you how to use five powerful principles for making the best possible decisions everywhere you go. He is the host of *Ask the Ethics Guy!* on Bloomberg Businessweek online's management channel and has written many ethics columns there.

He regularly gives keynote addresses to businesses, schools, and professional associations across the country. His clients include the National Football League, Northrop Grumman, the Investment Management Consultants Association, the International Foundation of Employee Benefit Plans, the Association of Test Publishers, Vistakon/Johnson & Johnson, the U.S. National Guard (South Carolina Division), the American Association of Collegiate Registrars and Admissions Officers, Help Desk International, Pri-Med, the colleges of business of Eastern Michigan University and the University of North Dakota, and over three hundred other leading groups.

You have seen Dr. Weinstein on a wide range of CNN programs, including *Anderson Cooper 360*, *American Morning*, *The Situation Room*, *Reliable Sources*, *Issue #1*, *Open House*, *CNN Live Saturday*, *Your Money*, and *The Flip Side*. He has also been featured on NBC's *Today Show*, ABC's *Good Morning America*, Fox News Channel's *O'Reilly Factor* and *Fox and Friends*, Fox Business's *Cavuto*, *MSNBC Live*, CNBC's *Power Lunch*, Bloomberg Television, Headline News, CNN International, and WNYC's *Leonard Lopate Show*.

His previous books include *Is It Still Cheating If I Don't Get Caught?*, *Life Principles: Feeling Good by Doing Good*, and *What Should I Do? 4 Simple Steps to Making Better Decisions in Everyday Life*. His writings have appeared in, and he has been quoted or featured in, *The New York Times*, *USA Today*, *Family Circle*, *The Los Angeles Times*, *The Chicago Tribune*, *The Philadelphia Inquirer*, *Investor's Business Daily*, *Real Simple*, and the in-flight magazines of American Airlines, Delta Air Lines, US Airways, and United Airlines, as well as on MSNBC.com, ABCNews.com, Newsweek.com, CNN.com, FoxNews.com, and Bankrate.com.

He received a bachelor's degree in philosophy from Swarthmore College, a PhD in philosophy and bioethics from Georgetown University, a certificate in film production from New York University, and a National Fellowship in Leadership Development from the W. K. Kellogg Foundation in Battle Creek, Michigan. He lives in New York with his wife, Kristen Bancroft.

He has twice been selected as a Top5 Speaker in Management, by Speakers Platform, one of the leading speakers' bureaus in the United States.

Join the Movement!

Do you want to promote ethical intelligence where you work, in your personal relationships, and in the world at large?

Sign up at TheEthicsGuy.com for a free newsletter that will give you weekly tips on how to make ethically intelligent decisions, lead by example, and inspire others to be the best they can be.

Let's make ethical intelligence a worldwide phenomenon!

NEW WORLD LIBRARY is dedicated to publishing books and other media that inspire and challenge us to improve the quality of our lives and the world.

We are a socially and environmentally aware company, and we strive to embody the ideals presented in our publications. We recognize that we have an ethical responsibility to our customers, our staff members, and our planet.

We serve our customers by creating the finest publications possible on personal growth, creativity, spirituality, wellness, and other areas of emerging importance. We serve New World Library employees with generous benefits, significant profit sharing, and constant encouragement to pursue their most expansive dreams.

As a member of the Green Press Initiative, we print an increasing number of books with soy-based ink on 100 percent postconsumer-waste recycled paper. Also, we power our offices with solar energy and contribute to nonprofit organizations working to make the world a better place for us all.

Our products are available
in bookstores everywhere.
For our catalog, please contact:

New World Library
14 Pamaron Way
Novato, California 94949

Phone: 415-884-2100 or 800-972-6657
Catalog requests: Ext. 50
Orders: Ext. 52
Fax: 415-884-2199
Email: escort@newworldlibrary.com

To subscribe to our electronic newsletter, visit
www.newworldlibrary.com

HELPING TO PRESERVE OUR ENVIRONMENT

3,183 trees were saved

New World Library uses 100% postconsumer-waste recycled paper for our books whenever possible, even if it costs more. During 2010 this choice saved the following precious resources:

www.newworldlibrary.com

ENERGY	WASTEWATER	GREENHOUSE GASES	SOLID WASTE
22 MILLION BTU	600,000 GAL.	750,000 LB.	200,000 LB.

Environmental impact estimates were made using the Environmental Defense Fund Paper Calculator @ www.papercalculator.org.